CONTEMPORARY NATIVE AMERICAN COMMUNITIES
Stepping Stones to the Seventh Generation

Despite the strength and vibrancy of Native American people and nations today, the majority of publications on Native peoples still reflect a public perception that these peoples largely disappeared after 1890. This series is meant to correct that misconception and to fill the void that has been created by examining contemporary Native American life from the point of view of Native concerns and values. Books in the series cover topics that are of cultural and political importance to tribal and urban Native peoples and that affect their possibilities for survival.

SERIES EDITORS

Troy Johnson
American Indian Studies
California State University, Long Beach
Long Beach, CA 90840
trj@csulb.edu

Duane Champagne
American Indian Studies Center
3220 Campbell Hall, Box 951548
University of California, Los Angeles
Los Angeles, CA 90095
champagn@ucla.edu

BOOKS IN THE SERIES

Inuit, Whaling, and Sustainability, Milton M. R. Freeman, Ingmar Egede, Lyudmila Bogoslovskaya, Igor G. Krupnik, Richard A. Caulfield, and Marc G. Stevenson (1998)

Contemporary Native American Political Issues, edited by Troy Johnson (1999)

Contemporary Native American Cultural Issues, edited by Duane Champagne (1999)

Modern Tribal Development: Paths to Self-Sufficiency and Cultural Integrity in Indian Country, Dean Howard Smith (2000)

American Indians and the Urban Experience, edited by Susan Lobo and Kurt Peters (2000)

EDITORIAL BOARD

Modern Tribal Development

Paths to Self-Sufficiency and Cultural Integrity in Indian Country

Dean Howard Smith

A Division of
ROWMAN & LITTLEFIELD PUBLISHERS, INC.
Walnut Creek • Lanham • New York • Oxford

AltaMira Press
A Division of Rowman & Littlefield Publishers, Inc.
1630 North Main Street, # 367
Walnut Creek, CA 94596
http://www.altamirapress.com

Rowman & Littlefield Publishers, Inc.
4720 Boston Way
Lanham, MD 20706

12 Hid's Copse Road
Cumnor Hill, Oxford OX2 9JJ, England

Copyright © 2000 by AltaMira Press

British Library Cataloguing in Publication Information Available

Library of Congress Cataloging-in-Publication Data
Smith, Dean Howard, 1958–
  Modern tribal development : paths to self-sufficiency and cultural integrity in Indian
Country / Dean Howard Smith.
    p. cm. — (Contemporary Native American communities ; v. 4)
  Includes bibliographical references and index.
  ISBN 0-7425-0409-3 (cloth : alk. paper) — ISBN 0-7425-0410-7 (paper : alk. paper)
    1. Indians of North America—Politics and government. 2. Indians of North
America—Economic conditions. 3. Indians of North America—Government relations. 4.
Indian reservations—United States. 5. Self-determination, National—United States. 6.
Indian business enterprises—United States. 7. Economic development—United States. I.
Title. II. Series.

E98.T77 S55 2000
973'.0497—dc21   99-042234

Printed in the United States of America

⊗™ The paper used in this publication meets the minimum requirements of American
National Standard for Information Sciences—Permanence of Paper for Printed Library
Materials, ANSI/NISO Z39.48–1992.

In memory of my parents, without whose support and guidance I would not have traveled the journey, this work is devoted to the people of the First Nations and the seventh generation to come. May the dawn's sun greet you smiling.

Contents

Preface

This work stems from a decade's worth of projects and activities. It combines field and primary research with academic study and teaching concerning Indian Country. Some background is necessary in detailing the nature of this work.

The Center for American Indian Economic Development (CAIED) is an entity in the College of Business Administration at Northern Arizona University whose mission is to provide technical assistance to tribes and businesses on the twenty-one reservations located in Arizona. The technical assistance provided includes everything from helping with business plans to developing computerized accounting systems to holding prebusiness workshops. These services are available to any reservation resident or any tribal entity. During the years of its existence, the center has helped many ongoing and fledgling businesses improve their profitability. The center houses an extensive library concerning technical issues in Indian Country and publishes a Web site informing subscribers of upcoming events and important issues. For information, contact CAIED, Box 15066, Northern Arizona University, Flagstaff, AZ 86011-5066.

During the past several years I have worked with the center on several projects, some of which are detailed in this volume and all of which have provided insight. These projects are important for this work because they provide an understanding of the complexities facing Native American businesses. Issues of trust land, water scarcity, and tribal interference all come to the forefront. Capital funding and labor supply problems raise their ugly heads. The practical aspects of these projects, and the ensuing issues, helped me move away from a purely theoretical background.

A second program with which I was involved is the National Executive Education Program for Native American Leadership (NEEPNAL). This program, initially funded by the Pew Charitable Trusts, is a joint project between Northern Arizona and Harvard Universities. NEEPNAL aimed at increasing the cultural integrity and sovereignty of the Native American Nations, using the means of economic development, leading to tribal self-determination and self-sufficiency. All NEEPNAL research and field projects are conducted at the request of tribal governments with tribal input and/or oversight.

Recognizing that economic development on reservations differs significantly from economic development elsewhere, NEEPNAL aims to develop both economic and institutional educational materials and workshops specifically aimed at the legal, sociological, cultural, and economic realities of the reservation. Staff researchers with extensive background in these matters explain the distinctions between Native American societies and mainstream society, thus allowing NEEPNAL to furnish relevant material and education to tribal leaders and educators so that the First Nations can and will become vital economies, thereby leading to cultural integrity, self-determination, and self-sufficiency. This is the driving force behind the goals and efforts of NEEPNAL.

I developed the background material for this book while I was conducting field visits to various reservations across the country. The interviews and lessons from these trips are detailed in this volume.

I also gathered background for this work from courses that I have taught. It is often said that you never really know a topic until you teach it. This is especially true in this case! Two courses on the economic development of the reservations and one course on public policy analysis provided plentiful background for the material contained herein. But much more important was the opportunity to work with dedicated students as each researched her or his own project. These projects varied from tourism development for Tuba City to the Hualapai Nation's constitution reform to developing entrepreneurial interest beginning with K-12 education. Directing these disparate research studies provided me with an opportunity to move outside internally focused scopes of interest. Several of my students have gone on to become important leaders in Indian Country.

Among the sources listed in the references, three works and one collection of papers have been of vital importance. The work edited by Stephen Cornell and Joseph Kalt, *What Can Tribes Do?* provides practical details on several institutional matters facing tribes. As the title suggests, this is a positive work for tribes searching for self-determination. Robert White's work, *Tribal Assets*, similarly provides positive examples of successful businesses on four reservations. *The Nations Within*, by Vine Deloria and Clifford Lytle, provides a detailed understanding of sovereignty issues. Lastly, the collection of papers available from the Harvard Project on American Indian Economic Development is indispensable reading for understanding the possibilities, and the problems, of Indian Country.

Background for this work also comes from a very personal source. Perhaps my earliest memory is of my father sitting me down for a conversation and explaining our family heritage and the importance of that heritage. I also remember the funny stories and problems inherent in any mixed marriage. My mother experienced difficulties and some humorous moments trying to understand the intense matriarchal structure of the Mohawks. Although my father's father left the reserve in the early 1930s, and we only ventured back once early in my life for a family gathering, that first lesson in life has always pushed me toward my current task.

Parts of this work have been modified from previously published academic papers. Chapter 4 on the development model and Chapter 9 on the Rosebud Sioux come from the paper "Native American Economic Development: A Modern Approach" published in the *Review of Regional Studies*. Chapters 1, 5, and 6 detailing social compatibility theory and the interplay between cultural integrity and economic development come from the paper "The Issue of Compatibility between Cultural Integrity, and Economic Development among Native American Tribes" published in the *American Indian Culture and Research Journal*. Chapter 8, concerning designing development plans, was also published in slightly different form in the *American Indian Culture and Research Journal*. Chapters 3 and 7 discussing the pre-contact societies and the relationship between the environment and human culture were initially developed in "Bridging TEK and Science to Create a New Environmental Society" in the forthcoming proceedings from the Bridging Traditional Ecological Knowledge and Ecosystem Science conference. Chapter 10 is taken from a teaching case in the Harvard series mentioned above. The author gratefully thanks the publishers for allowing this material to be incorporated in this volume.

As I already mentioned, this work was not produced in the isolation of an ivory tower. Many people helped with the research and understandings contained herein. Several contacts in Indian Country were particularly helpful: Marylin Enfield, Mike Her Many Horses, Waylon Honga, Matthew Foster, Jonathan Speier, and Joe Flies-Away. They provided insightful and open conversation concerning the goals and hopes of their people. At the center, Joan Timeche, Hamp Merrill, Sharon Singer, and Arlene Laughter coordinated, directed, and facilitated much of the original fieldwork. In addition, they provided many hours of brainstorming. Under the NEEPNAL category come Steve Cornell, Joe Kalt, and Joe Walka for having the inspiration to design the program. Ron Trosper, Jon Ozmun, Ted Helmer, Linda Stratton, and Jerry Conover at NAU provided much discussion and cheering. Duane Champagne of UCLA and an anonymous referee pointed me in the direction of digging deeper into social changes than I had initially imagined. More recently, Joe Anderson has become a valued coauthor and partner. Carole Goldberg of UCLA, Keith James of Colorado State University, and Ron Trosper provided platforms for developing the materials included herein by organizing important conferences. Of course, I must thank the many students from my classes for providing worthy sounding boards and writing—typically—worthy papers. My lifelong friend Stephen Gregg deserves thanks for his many hours of arguments—most incurring long distance telephone charges—concerning Indian Country and the development process. (Stephen still disagrees with most of the ideas contained herein! Maybe when he reads it, he will finally be convinced.) Lastly, but certainly most importantly, I want to thank my wife, Steffie, for her emotional support and for understanding my travels away from home and accepting the many nights when she slept alone while I, listening to Dylan and Marley, worked on this project. My love and thanks.

Introduction

❧

The Potentials
for Indian Country

N o wagons were circled. No cavalry blared its bugle. The air was not permeated with the stench of gunpowder and death nor was the silence
shattered by the wails of starving and dying women and children. Rather, a
secret land deal was made between representatives of the U.S. government
and some Indians. Those individuals affected by the settlement had little, if
any, input in the process. The announcement of the settlement brought rage,
disbelief, misunderstanding, and confusion. Complaints were logged and
threats were made. But this time, ironically, the Native Americans were getting land and the non-Indians were wailing.

In November 1992 a public announcement was made concerning an
agreement in principle on a land dispute between the Navajo Nation, the
Hopi Tribe, and the federal government. The dispute, which has a long
and storied history, dates back to 1880. The announcement of the settlement brought vociferous reactions from a wide variety of people either
directly or indirectly affected by the resulting land swap.

The scenario was interesting to anyone familiar with the issues burning
in Indian Country because it included several new and exciting aspects.
First, the Navajo Nation and Hopi Tribe were negotiating in good faith
with the goal of reaching an agreement on a very controversial conflict.
Second, the two tribes were equal partners with the federal government
in the negotiations and settlement language. And, most importantly, the
two tribes were negotiating from a stance of self-determined choice. Both
tribal leaders, Chairman Vernon Maseyesva of the Hopi and President
Peterson Zah of the Navajo, explained their reasoning and expectations
from positions of strength and knowledge. They understood the issues,

goals, and aims of the policy. They also understood the severe problem areas of the agreement in principle. Both spoke of economic, political, and spiritual sovereignty for their respective peoples. They also spoke of respect for each other and for mainstream society.

This book addresses the path toward self-determination and self-sufficiency taken by the First Nations within the framework of the United States. The settlement process for the resolution of the Navajo–Hopi land dispute is stalled and continues to defy solution. The land dispute stems from a partitioning of the former Navajo–Hopi Joint Use Area in 1975. Because of the partitioning, over 10,000 Navajos and Hopis found themselves living on the wrong side of the line: Navajos living on Hopi land and vice versa. Accordingly, the U.S. government was responsible for relocating families on the wrong side of the line. By 1992 over $300 million had been spent, but some families, primarily Navajo, refused to leave their homesteads. In order to arrive at a final solution, the agreement in principle included the purchase and transfer of thousands of acres of private land and thousands of acres of public land to the two tribes. But that issue is not the focus of this book. Emily Benedek (1992) fully details the history of the conflict, and many news articles detail the aftermath of the agreement in principle. In this volume I explain how self-determination and self-sufficiency can, and in many cases have, become a reality for the First Nations.

The United States is a heterogeneous mixture of diverse cultures and regions. Differences in cultural norms, languages, traditions, and religions are often viewed as an energy driving the country to the forefront of the global economy, thereby providing incentives for other countries to follow the U.S. example. The aboriginal population in the United States also includes a large number of distinct cultures. These populations face severe social and economic problems stemming from past mistreatment by the federal government. As a result, many of the distinct values and traditional practices of the Native American tribes are threatened. But hope persists, and cultural, social, and economic progress is being made. A manifest imperative in Indian Country is maintaining Native cultures and strengthening their sovereign powers. One of the methods of achieving this goal is developing tribal resources within a cultural context.

This work maintains that economic development is a means to the end of sustaining tribal character. It is vital to formulate all development plans with an eye toward how they impact the overall society. Only when the individual tribe has control of its resources and sustains its identity as a distinct civilization does economic development make sense; otherwise, the tribe must choose between economic development and cultural integrity. A common misconception sees conflict between maintaining a tribe's cultural heritage and pursuing increased economic activity on the reservation. However, a main purpose of this work is to show that economic development increases the potential for strengthening and developing tribal culture.

Historically, federal Indian policy aimed at reducing the cultures and sovereign powers of Native American tribes. Policies such as allotment, boarding schools, termination, and BIA (Bureau of Indian Affairs) management have all attempted to assimilate Native Americans into mainstream society. Countering these policies was the Constitution's recognizing the Indian Tribes as the equals of other sovereign nations, which led to treaties, relocations, reservations, and the like aimed at maintaining the Indian populations as distinct societies. However, all of these policies have failed. The dire poverty facing Indians both on and off reservations is clear evidence of the failure of these past policies. Continued economic deprivation on the reservations diminishes the Native cultures; however, if tribes are successful in their new economic development plans, their cultural integrity will be strengthened.

The influence of past policies on the cultures of Native America helped create the current circumstances facing reservation populations. A new social compatibility paradigm explains that culture is a dynamically moving set of social subsystems and that when any one subsystem is knocked out of equilibrium with the others, then the whole set of subsystems must adjust to the new environment. This knowledge also allows an understanding of how the various subsystems need to be adjusted to bring forth a productive and growing culture based on traditions and modern realities.

The Nixon era brought about a new ideal for Indian policy: self-determination.[1] Since then, improvements *have* been made, but the various controversies concerning gaming facilities show that true self-determination has not been fully realized. Thus three interwoven questions arise: (1) how do tribes maintain their cultural individuality and secure their cultural integrity, (2) how do tribes develop their sovereign rights as stipulated in the Constitution and laws of the United States and the treaties, and, most importantly, (3) how do tribes become fully self-determined and self-sufficient, thereby securing their rights and cultures? This book focuses on the importance of economic development as a means to answering these questions.[2]

Development theories have recently begun to understand the distinction between simply providing infrastructure and capital improvements and a more holistic approach toward community development. In an article entitled "Native American Economic Development: A Modern Approach" (1994a) I used the paradigm developed by Jane Jacobs (1984) to study the Rosebud Sioux Reservation from a community development perspective in terms of economic activity, cultural and community interactions, and a long-term time horizon. Robert White (1990) provides narrative descriptions of how five reservations have merged economic development with community development. These reservations are utilizing rising income to regain their self-sufficiency, when that term is used in a holistic sense and not simply a monetary one. Coming from a slightly different angle, ethnobotanist Mark Plotkin (1993) argues that potential profits from the use of indigenous medicines can—and do—restore tribal interest in traditional medicines, dances, and ceremonies among the tribes in the Amazon rain forest. Thus, in keeping with a dynamic system of social compatibility, as discussed below, this book studies how traditional indigenous cultures can merge with economic development to provide vibrant and progressive cultures for the reservation populations.

In order to accomplish this goal, part 1 takes an overview perspective. The overall structure of a social system is addressed instead of the specific details of operationalizing the process. Part 2 provides examples of both methods and processes of putting development plans into action. Since each tribe has individual cultural norms, traditions, and goals, a program for any one tribe may be completely inappropriate for another tribe. Thus this work provides an overall pattern to guide precise planning practices.

Recent approaches to problems facing Native American reservation economies address practical solutions to severe poverty and associated socioeconomic ills while recognizing cultural and sovereignty issues as opposed to simply listing the historical causes of these issues. I have been involved with undertakings such as the Harvard Project on American Indian Economic Development and Northern Arizona University's Center for American Indian Economic Development, which focus on pragmatic solutions to specific development issues; a joint project of Northern Arizona and Harvard Universities, the National Executive Education Program for Native American Leadership (NEEPNAL), which works with tribal governments and enterprises in educating leadership and designing task-specific solutions; the Center for American Indian Economic Development (CAIED), a state agency, which aids individuals and tribes with economic development activities within Arizona. At Northern Arizona University CAIED holds workshops and conducts consulting projects. Several other public and private, local and national enterprises are also active in aiding tribes and reservation businesses.

The reservation population in the United States is approaching 2 million, the resources available to reservation economies are becoming more valuable, and the education levels on reservations are rising. Besides recent advances in terms of potential, the ideology of both the federal government and, most importantly, tribal governments has shifted from a paternalistic approach to one of self-sufficiency and self-determination.

As we will see in the chapters that follow, the causes and potential for the recent changes can lead Native America through the twenty-first century with social and economic frameworks that are vastly improved over the ones that exist today. In order to do so, Native Americans are taking a proactive stance toward their problems and concerns (such as the Navajo and Hopi leaders attempted). In particular, tribal governments have opened their institutions to the concepts of development and progress. However, development and progress are not to be thought of as simply merging with the mainstream economy and society. No indeed. The successes of Native America are to be evaluated, measured, and appraised within the context of the individual tribe's cultural and social makeup.

This work focuses on the Indian Nations in the United States today, which include several hundred identifiable cultures. In addition, several reservations are made up of amalgamations of several tribes. The overriding concern of this book is that these cultures remain identifiable and distinct. Thus the evaluation of any development prospectus must be made within the dictums of the individual indigenous social structure. Appraisal is not to consider the mainstream society's goals and system; nor is it to be measured according to some pan-Indian framework. Each culture is distinct and must be allowed to make its own rules and regulations in the context of social norms and mores.

Although this work focuses on the indigenous peoples of the United States, other indigenous peoples can use many of the lessons. In particular, the second half of this book applies to aboriginal peoples across the globe. Since Canada is most closely linked to the United States in terms of Indian policy, the specifics are most appropriate. But the overall development paradigm presented is also appropriate for indigenous peoples under the control of conquesting peoples. In fact, most of the development paradigm is also appropriate to mainstream society, wherever that society is located. The important point is that the prototype be adapted to the local social system.

Many issues of importance in Indian Country are beyond the experience of the author and thus lie outside the scope of this work. For example, nonreservation-based Native populations are not directly addressed, but, as just mentioned, many of the lessons in it can be adapted to them. Issues of the allotment period and its aftermath, although of vital importance in places such as Oklahoma, also lie outside the current discussion.

The ideas of self-determination and self-sufficiency (or perhaps the renewal of feeling associated with them) are flowing throughout Indian Country. After several centuries of dictatorial edicts from the invading populations, Native America is currently experiencing a renewed vision of possibilities. This book focuses on those potentials. Modern Native America can, and hopefully will, become a source of ideas, products, and insight into the human condition for leaders around the globe, but only if Native leaders take proactive steps to ensure the future of the aboriginal cultures.

TERMS AND DEFINITIONS

A work of this sort must rely on a series of definitions that differ slightly from common usage. In order to provide narrative variation, several terms are used synonymously.

The terms Native American, American Indians, Indians, indigenous peoples, and people of the First Nations are used interchangeably to indicate people who trace their ancestry and cultural identification to those peoples indigenous to lands now included in the United States.

There are serious ideological arguments concerning some of these terms. For example, during extended committee meetings during the design of the new Applied Indigenous Studies program (or whatever the final name will be) at my home institution, many hours were spent simply discussing the name of the program. Similar issues have come up in regard to the various descriptors for Americans of African ancestry. There are also legal and political issues concerning degree of lineage—who qualifies as an Indian under a series of regulations? Three examples make the distinction clear.

According to federal equal opportunity and affirmative action laws, I qualify as an Indian due to community recognition of this fact, which is backed up by a "degree of blood" qualification. However, I am not a recognized tribal member in the United States, since my family comes from a reservation in Canada.

Tribal constitutions specify the degree of blood required for membership. Depending on the political goals of the tribe, the degree may vary. Tribal membership is important for a variety of reasons, such as voting opportunities, site lease preference, and per capita payments.

Federal regulations stipulate that any individual selling arts and crafts as a Native American must be a recognized member of a recognized tribe. Thus the definition becomes hazy. A person with one-fourth quantum blood in one tribe may be able to sell "Indian" arts and crafts, but another individual of three-eighths quantum blood may be precluded from doing so, since tribal membership requires one-half blood quantum. Since this book focuses on the development of the reservation populations, these arguments lie outside the realm of current discussion.

Similarly, the term tribe will be used as an overall term. Other terms are Nation or reservation. Specific distinctions are useful, but the overall usage will be synonymous. The Hualapai Nation is the political agent governing the Hualapai Tribe on the Hualapai Reservation. Not all tribal members live on the reservation, nor, as indicated above, do all persons having ancestry within the Hualapai peoples have tribal membership. Further confusing the matter is the fact that some reservations are made up of peoples from more than one tribe. For instance, the Fort Belknap Reservation has members from two tribes, and the Warm Springs Reservation has members from three tribes. Therefore, the terms tribe, nation, and reservation are interchangeable, except when used in proper names. The term band is relevant for many reservations on the West Coast. Alaska Natives and their communities introduce other terms.

Tribes and reservation populations are designations based on federal regulation and anthropological niches; however, the primary allegiance of any individual is commonly to some other designation. For instance, extended families, clans, villages, and bands are often the focus of an individual, whereas the legal designation combines several of these disparate groups to form one tribe.

These issues complicate any work addressing a general framework for development. However, in this volume I do not make any "pan-Indian" prescription. Rather, the specific goals, aims, mores, and norms of a specific band, clan, tribe, nation, or reservation—which often conflict with one another—can adopt the general paradigm that is presented in these pages.

FINAL INTRODUCTORY THOUGHTS

The current state of many First Nations is severely troubled. The social and cultural frameworks of these identifiable societies are facing severe problems. Federal policies of the past have left the economies of these nations deeply impoverished. However, two hundred years of conflicting federal policy aimed at forcing Indians to become part of the mainstream and at the same time isolating the populations in order to maintain the sovereignty of the tribes has not extinguished the vitality of indigenous cultures. Tribal membership is not simply a fact of history, as it is with many second- and third-generation Americans. Tribal membership involves knowledge of the tribe's cultural history, language, spirituality, traditions, and social system. In spite of past federal policies and atrocities, these cultures are still identifiable, but they are in trouble because of the severe economic hardships present on most reservations.

For those interested in one explanation of the causes of the conditions faced by many reservation populations, Ward Churchill's (1997) work provides an absorbing read. Although his perspective is rather one-sided, he provides a thought-provoking interpretation of history.

A holistic understanding of the importance of cultural integrity merged with the concepts of economic development and self-determination shows a pathway to cultural growth and economic self-sufficiency. The First Nations are poised to enter the global economy and are bearers of philosophies necessary for future development of the global environment.

An advertisement by the American Indian College Fund[3] pointed out four areas in which "traditional American Indian thinking applies" to modern problems: environment, family structure, greed, and international turmoil. However, the purpose of the advertisement was to raise donations for the fund in order to increase education rates on the reservations. Education is aimed at improving the job skills of the students and increasing their knowledge of tribal heritage and traditions. Economic development without concomitant principles of cultural and social identity simply leads to consumerism, a result being disavowed within the mainstream economy as environmental, family values, and other issues become more pressing. Cultural identification without economic development is not self-sufficient and diminishes as disposable resources are reduced and pure survival becomes the individual's goal. But when the two are viewed as synergetic, growth of the social and cultural aspects of the individual and tribe as a whole is possible.

Plotkin (1993, chapters 6, 9) points out several important recent observations of relevance here. First, disruption of the equilibrium among cultural subsystems results in severe problems down the road. For instance, when missionaries introduced guns, Indians lost their traditional hunting methods, and when the shotgun shells ran out, they became beggars. However, Plotkin shows how the various cultural subsystems can be developed to provide a growing and sustainable society with improved economic activity and sustained traditions.

After working with a particular rain forest tribe for over a decade, Plotkin provided a plant medicine handbook in the local language. He also helped develop a profit-sharing and investment strategy with several pharmaceutical companies for continued research. A result of all this has been a shaman apprenticeship program for several tribes where no apprentices were previously in training. He concludes:

> I feel strongly that this effort has helped validate their culture in the eyes of the Indians. Prior to this work, the Tiros had only one book written in their language: the holy Bible. This research constitutes a true partnership between Western and Indian cultures; both share in any potential material benefits, but more important, this approach to ethnobotany helps the indigenous peoples understand the potential global importance of a fundamental aspect of their culture. (p. 287)

Thus Plotkin shows how the ideas in this book can be applied in practice: economic development and traditional beliefs can work together to provide a vibrant and developing culture. The cultural integrity of indigenous peoples can be enhanced by this development if the subsystems are allowed to reach a higher level of equilibrium, and this depends on allowing the indigenous populations to make their own decisions concerning their resources.

Progress in Indian Country will not be simple. The existing situation is desperate, but an extended time horizon involving the seventh generation shows that progress can and will occur. Specific plans of action need to be formulated. Education and job creation must occur. Resource development needs to be enacted, within cultural norms and ideals. Projects such as NEEPNAL, CAIED, First Nations Financial Project, the National Center for American Indian Enterprise and Development, and local business organizations need to continue their dedicated efforts in research and assistance.[4] Managerial skills must be developed. Federal policy must be redesigned to allow for true self-determination. And tribal governments must become more stable and responsible. But progress *is* being made and will continue. The future of self-determined, identifiable Indian societies shows positive potential for creating communities of opportunity and cultural vitality.

NOTES

1. Previous recognition is evidenced by the Indian Reorganization Act of 1934. However, the power of the BIA and the cookie cutter IRA constitutions did not lead to self-determination or cultural and sovereign integrity. Of course, some of the resulting legislation was passed during the Ford administration.

2. Other matters, such as constitutional and institutional reform, are equally important but are not a major focus of this work. Joseph Kalt, *The Redefinition of Property Rights in American Indian Reservations: A Comparative Analysis of Native American Economic Development* (Cambridge: Harvard Project on American Indian Economic Development, John F. Kennedy School of Government, 1987); Stephen Cornell and Joseph Kalt, "Pathways from Poverty: Economic Development and Institution-Building on American Indian Reservations," *American Indian Culture and Research Journal* 14, no. 3 (1990): 89–125; Cornell and Kalt, *Where's the Glue? Institutional Bases of American Indian Economic Development* (Cambridge: Harvard Project on American Indian Economic Development, John F. Kennedy School of Government, 1991); and Cornell and Kalt, "Reloading the Dice: Improving the Chances for Economic Development on American Indian Reservations," in *What Can Tribes Do? Strategies and Institutions in American Indian Economic Development*, ed. Stephen Cornell and Joseph Kalt (Los Angeles: American Indian Studies Center, 1992) focus on some of these issues.

3. "A Sane, Rational Argument for Giving the Entire Country Back to the Indians," advertisement for the American Indian College Fund, *U.S. News and World Report*, October 4, 1993, p. 84c.

4. See *Indian Business and Management*, December 1991, p. 12, for a listing of the Native American Chambers of Commerce and similar organizations. This magazine is published by the National Center for American Indian Enterprise Development.

PART ONE

A PARADIGM FOR DEVELOPMENT

The first seven chapters of this book set the stage for understanding the community development process within a Native American context. The foundation of the development process is based on the social compatibility framework and the cycle of economic growth.

Understanding how social systems evolve over time—not necessarily toward the better—provides a framework for discussing a movement from the status quo to hope and realization within the populations of the First Nations. The overwhelming intrusion of white American society into the lives of the First Nations severely disrupted our extensively developed and complex social systems.

Recent changes in the direction of federal interference allow our people an opportunity to rebuild. The main focus of this work is community development based on a viable economic subsystem. Thus it is imperative to understand how economic subsystems evolve and grow over time. The cycle of growth model—although not requiring all phases—provides an intellectual structure for us to articulate the process by which Native Americans can fit modern economic activity into a culturally based community development program.

Culturally designed economic development programs can also cycle back to help sustain and further invigorate Native cultures. As with the very process of economic growth, this circular argument fits well with First Nations' worldviews. As the economic system grows, other aspects of society can flourish. Language and educational programs can be developed and expanded, which in turn will provide additional opportunities for economic activity.

Combining an understanding of social evolution and economic development with Native American worldviews concerning the environment allows for recognition of additional potential. Not only can these lessons be appropriate for developing the First Nations populations, but they can also be applied to mainstream issues concerning environmental degradation.

The theoretical background discussed in the following chapters has been augmented by extensive fieldwork with tribes across the United States. The input from Native American practitioners and tribal leaders provides evidence that the paradigm presented in these chapters can be used to develop community plans.

1

❧

A Social
Compatibility Paradigm

Distinguishing between maintaining and developing cultural integrity and developing the economy of a society is vitally important to our current purposes. By "culture" I mean the code of conduct and code of values defining the distinction between one people and another. For instance, aspects of culture include the nuances of language, spiritual beliefs, traditions, reverence for family and tribe, and cross-generational viewpoints.

The economy, on the other hand, is the production mechanism of society. Although certain political campaigns have suggested that society is the economy, the opposite is true. The economic system merely helps society become itself, and the lack of an economic system adds to the downward spiral of the social structure. Economic activity is not the end result of anything; rather, it is the engine that drives society to higher culture levels.

The quest is to design an economic structure that allows the rest of the society to maintain its cultural integrity and develop new and improved methods of living. In many cases, the cultural issues outweigh economic activity.

Certainly some tribes, or tribal factions, have taken formal stands of *not* desiring any part in developing their economies along the pathways of mainstream society. These include the Hopi, Hualapai, and Havasupai Tribes in Arizona. The Hopis have decided to forgo potentially large tourist revenues in order to maintain the integrity of their religious ceremonies. The Hualapai have closed off a large portion of their reservation to "outsiders" because they want to live in their traditional manner (De Mente 1988, 75). The Havasupai turned down potentially immense revenues and other niceties of "modern society" from uranium mining.[1] In each case, tribal leadership held the view that the benefits from developing the potential market were outweighed by the conflicting interests of maintaining and substantiating tribal traditions. Continuing the University of Chicago–style parlance, the opportunity costs of cultural interference and disruption outweigh the goods and services gained from additional income. The Hopi feel that outside participation in and exploitation of their ceremonies demeans the significance of these very spiritual events. The Hualapai, similarly, feel that intrusion into their traditional ways of living undermines and detracts from their communing with the natural forces of the universe. The Havasupai—as well as the Hualapai—feel that mining the uranium deposits desecrates the Mother. Indeed, there was some discussion that the 1990 flood that struck the village of Supai was punishment upon the Havasupai by the Spirit for even considering a mining operation. Therefore, for these three tribes—as well as many others—the seeming conflict between cultural integrity and economic development reduced potential increases in personal and tribal income. But each tribe is engaging in other economic development strategies. Therefore, these choices fall within the realm of self-determined action and as such cannot be denied. Thus Barbara Ward (1962) correctly argues that *economic* development is not necessarily synonymous with *cultural* development.

Another example helps to bring this point further into the open. During classroom discussion,[2] one student mentioned the following. He visited his grandparents' home on the Navajo Reservation every weekend and returned to the university during the week. He said, "Out there they have everything they need. They have sheep and corn and everything. They don't want any development. I come back to the city [Flagstaff], and there is all this noise. You can't think. I go home, and I'm comfortable. Why do we need any development?" Thus those tribes desiring to live in traditional ways, *and are able to sustain that lifestyle,* are making rational choices concerning their resources: this is the very definition of self-determination.

Other tribes, however, are interested in developing their economies as a means toward the end of self-determination. In other words, developing natural and human resources can strengthen their culture. For instance, Marilyn Enfield of Apache Aerospace stated that her goal as general manager is to be "profit driven, but balanced with Apache values."[3] Reaching this goal included activities ranging from testifying to Congress to participating in Sunrise Dances, and from negotiating with McDonnell-Douglas to meeting individually with traditional council members and explaining, in Apache, how Apache Aerospace could help lead the tribe achieve true self-determination.

The point is that economic development can help tribes become self-sufficient without undermining their cultural integrity. As incomes rise, the tribe becomes less dependent on federal aid, and this leads to true self-determination. As tribes truly begin to manage their resources, they can maintain and strengthen their cultural values. As development occurs, tribal members have an opportunity for increased pride in their culture and heritage, and the individual civilization prospers in more ways than rising income. As a counterexample, consider for a moment an economy continuing the problems currently present on reservations. The likelihood of such a society maintaining its cultural integrity in the face of poverty, alcoholism, malnutrition, and the like is rather low.

Additionally, maintaining cultural integrity does not necessitate returning to pre-Columbian economies—not even the Havasupai desire to do so.[4] Rather, the behavioral characteristics that make an individual an Apache or a Navajo or a Mohawk are maintained *and developed*. As Native Americans' standard of living rises, more resources are available to them for developing and maintaining these cultural elements. For example, the Navajo Nation is facing a diminishing stock of both "singers"[5] and weavers. As the Navajo economy develops, there will be resources available to pay for ceremonies, and as the market for woven rugs develops, there will be income from weaving, thus increasing the number of both singers and weavers, which bolsters the cultural integrity of the tribe.

This by no means implies that economic development should be engaged in simply for the purpose of improving income. Development for the sake of development is not being suggested, rather, development as a means toward a well-defined end. Clearly, there are many potential negative aspects, such as those mentioned concerning the Hopi, Hualapai, and Havasupai, when considering development plans. Well-designed tribal plans and institutions can aid in avoiding some of the pitfalls of inappropriate development activities.

For instance, Paul Nissenbaum and Paul Shadle (1992) designed a land-use planning board for the Puyallup Tribe that included a definitive process of looking at impacts on the salmon fisheries of *any* proposed land use. In other words, the tribe has prioritized the various subsystems of the culture and has deemed the spiritual aspects of the fisheries to be more important than simple dollars. Thus the economic subsystem has been made compatible with the spiritual subsystem. This cultural compatibility of the subsystems is vital for a progressing society.

Clearly, conflicts between culture and economic activity can arise. Past development strategies either were conducted by outside interests for the benefit of outsiders or were designed with the goal of assimilating the tribes into the mainstream capitalist-style economy. The potential gains from activities designed by and for Native Americans need to be rethought with a view toward reducing the negative aspects of those activities. These gains include increasing opportunities for and interest by tribal members in their traditions, heritage, language, and identity. Reducing the negative aspects includes designing environmentally sound and culturally sensitive activities.

Culture is the way of living developed and transmitted by a group of people to subsequent generations (Harris and Moran 1991). Included in culture are artifacts, beliefs, ethics, moral and other values, and underlying assumptions that allow people to make sense of themselves and their environment. Culture is "the software of the human mind" (Hofstede 1992, 12). Edward Devereux states that culture includes

> shared bits of knowledge, techniques, symbols with special shared meaning, tools and other significant objects, normative standards, and even goals. Culture, in this sense, thus represents the shared property of the members of the social system: the items which comprise it are all potentially teachable or transferable to some new member of the system. (1961, 26)

The term cultural integrity implies maintaining and supporting the shared property of a society deemed essential for identification as a member of that culture. It also includes the adaptation of this shared property as time passes within the context of the shared code of values and conduct.

Compatibility between economic activity and tribal goals is highlighted in comments by John Bowannie (1992), president of Cochiti Community Development Corporation and former governor of the Cochiti Pueblo. He distinguishes between culture and tradition. Tradition comprises activities that describe the heritage of the tribe, including religious and ceremonial activities. Culture incorporates the traditions with other aspects of life such as work and regulations. Therefore, traditions are aspects of the culture that are steeped in history. Bowannie further explains that while it may be difficult to merge traditional behavior with successful competition in a market economy, it is not impossible. Furthermore, some aspects of the culture can be developed and improved when the traditions and values of the tribe are merged with an evolving economy.

Economic development, on the other hand, is simply the utilization and development of the natural and human resources available to produce marketable goods and services to exchange with other segments of the global economy for other goods and services. My purpose in this chapter is to show that economic development can be a means toward the end of securing cultural integrity and allowing cultural development.[6]

Adam Smith (1776) contended that economic development is simply a means to an end and not an end in itself. In stating that consumption was the means and end of production, he realized that the production of goods and services (i.e., economic development) was accomplished because society has an interest in acquiring an ever higher standard of living and is willing to work toward that end. Therefore, developing the economy by utilizing and developing the available resources is the method by which any society develops and maintains its culture. In Chicago-style economic parlance, the term consumption includes not only tangible goods and services but also the time necessary to participate in cultural activities and leisure.

Talcott Parsons extends the idea that economic production is not the final end of any society:

> The goal of the economy is not simply the production of income for the utility of an aggregate of individuals. It is the maximization of production relative to the whole complex of institutionalized value-systems and functions of the society, and its subsystems. As a matter of fact, if we view the goal of the economy as defined strictly by socially structured goals, it becomes inappropriate even to refer to utility at this level in terms of individual preference lists. . . . The categories of wealth, utility, and income are states or properties of the social systems and their units and do not apply to the personality of the individual except *through* the social system. (1957, 146)

Indeed, according to Parsons, the cultural aspects of a society even help define the individual's preference structure. For example, the mainstream society places heavy emphasis on individuality and financial success and thus also on formal education and occupational choice. Most indigenous societies, however, place more emphasis on family and spiritual harmony, thereby placing more significance on informal education and interactive ceremonies.

Also worthy of note is the idea that developing a society's economic resources does not necessarily imply that the culture is developing. Ward, in discussing the development of Western Europe and North America, notes that

> I do not know whether one would say of this new society that it is demonstrably happier. Sometimes I think people wonder whether it can be said to be more civilized. But there is one thing which is absolutely certain. It is sensationally richer. (1962, 17)

Devereux continues his discussion by asserting that economic production techniques need to match the remainder of the society's cultural structure:

> Parsons has argued that a familistic system such as that in classical China would be drastically dysfunctional in an industrial capitalistic society such as our own. In effect, commitments made in one area of the social structure restrict alternatives in others . . . there are structural imperatives peculiar to each specific type of society, imperatives relevant to the structural compatibility and mutual articulation of the *various subsystems in the same society with each other*. (1961, 38; emphasis added)

The paradigm being developed here also indicates that culture is in ever evolving and fluid movement as the various subsystems constantly strive for compatibility. This point is developed further by Chandler Morse:

> A basic distinction is drawn between the *production* of wealth and income and their actual use for the attainment of system goals. This seems to mean

that there is conceived to be a basic distinction between (1) the allocation of resources and (2) the distribution of income. Economic theory treats these as two aspects of a single process. When Parsons implies that the former is the function of the Economy, the latter of the Polity, he is therefore making a sharp but perhaps important break with a well-established intellectual position. (1961, 125)

This break with previous theory is vital because the idea of progress needs recasting away from an assimilationist ideal toward Native American ideals—tribes need to be able to find their own levels of compatibility. This does not necessarily imply merely assimilating into an industrial capitalist economic system that does not mesh with the other subsystems.

Each tribe must decide which direction it will take, as well as which aspects of tradition are vital or evolving. Additionally, each tribe needs to formulate its own goals for economic activities. For example, the Grand Traverse Band reaches compatibility between subsystems by using the revenues from the gaming enterprise to fund governmental activities such as child care and buildings. The Warm Springs Reservation is using the profits from various activities for scholarships, housing, and substance abuse programs.[7] Whereas tribal enterprises and entrepreneurial activity must be competitive in the global or local marketplace, their goals in pursuing those activities may differ from those of non-Indian businesses. In this sense, progress can be defined as moving toward self-determination and self-sufficiency such that the tribal community is able to maintain those traditions deemed important and essential while evolving (not assimilating) other aspects of the culture. Thus, adhering to the code of values that makes a person Apache or Navajo or Mohawk is not in conflict with economic development activities when those activities are guided by that same code of values.

In conclusion, cultural development involves an ever evolving system of cultural subsystems, including the spiritual, economic, family, ceremonial, and others. This dynamic system and the compatibility among the various sectors defines not only the society as a whole but also the individuals within that society. The social compatibility paradigm dictates that these subsystems are always changing to bring about a compatible equilibrium. It is an understatement to describe the current equilibrium of Native American reservations as suboptimal. The main reason for the current situation is the fact that these societies have undergone drastic changes in several vital subsystems, but the changes were imposed changes from without, as opposed to a progressive change coming from within the existing culture.

A BRIEF APPLICATION TO INDIAN COUNTRY

The social theory being presented here can be used to explain how economic development can aid tribes in maintaining and developing their cultures. The following statement, supposedly made by Chief Seattle, helps explain our social paradigm: "And what will happen when we say good-by to the swift pony and the hunt? It will be the end of living and the beginning of survival" (Jeffers 1991, 20).[8]

Chief Seattle foretold the results of the reservation system in the United States and Canada. The disruption of a very profitable economic system, the end of the hunt in this case, clearly caused a downward spiral of the social system for tribes as they moved onto reservations. In many instances the move from the traditional lands to a distant reservation site completely destroyed the traditional economy. Even as the traditional governmental and spiritual structures were destroyed, Chief Seattle's foreboding came true as the various subsystems of the social structure reached a new level of compatibility. Given the lack of governance, economy, and spiritual sustenance, it is hardly surprising that many reservation populations simply survived—or worse.

Another aspect of Chief Seattle's comments further illustrates how our social theory works: the pony is a post-contact technology! Yet in the couple of centuries between the introduction of this technology, including the biological production of sufficient productive units, and Chief Seattle's comments, this new technology had permeated the social structures of many tribes. The equine-based economic and defense systems infiltrated the rest of the social structure as other subsystems reached a new level of compatibility with the increased profitability of the economic system and the increased effectiveness of the defense system.[9]

Chief Seattle's statement shows both aspects of our theory. In the first instance a disruption of the status quo can lead to a downward spiral of the social structure when an exogenous change moves the system out of equilibrium. On the other hand, a positive exogenous change can lead to improvements in other aspects of the social structure.

In later chapters I describe how and why Native American social systems have faltered in the face of two hundred years of federal policy and, for current purposes, how indigenous cultures can lead the Native American reservations toward a successful future by developing their economies. Developing reservation economies is vital to sustaining and developing Native American cultural identities.

The theory explains that culture is a dynamically moving set of social subsystems and that when any one subsystem is knocked out of equilibrium with the others, then the whole set of subsystems must adjust to the new environment. Subsystems can be described as involving sectors of the social fabric. For example, subsystems include the economic system, religious system, familial system, artistic system, and environmental system. An equilibrium is reached when the various subsystems reach a point of stasis. This by no means implies that the social structure has reached a point of unconstrained or even constrained optimization; rather, given the governing body of constraints, the system has reached a steady state.

NORGAARD'S COEVOLUTIONARY THEORY

Richard Norgaard (1994 and elsewhere) develops a body of thought based on "coevolution theory," which states that the various aspects of society coevolve in conjunction with the environment. Changes in the environment influence changes in the overall society and vice versa. One example involves the historical interactions among "Pests, Pesticides, Politics and Policy" (1994, 23ff.). As DDT and other pesticides were introduced to combat various pests, the pests became resistant, which led to the development of new pesticides. The environmental problems, including nontarget species effects, resulted in various political discussions and new policies.

Alternatively,

> in the coevolutionary paradigm, the environment determines the fitness of how people behave as guided by alternative ways of knowing, forms of social organization, and types of technologies. Yet at the same time, how people know, organize and use tools determines the fitness characteristics of an evolving environment. At any point in time, each determines the other. (Norgaard 1994, 46)

Norgaard argues that economic progress within Western culture, which has been extremely successful since 1600, and especially since the industrial revolution, came about because of the Judeo-Christian beliefs that humankind has governance over the Earth. "Many people operate on the *belief* that progress will occur through continued technological advance unless *scientifically* proven otherwise" (1994, 54). Belief in progress is the default assumption of modern Western culture. However, new realities have eroded faith in that assumption. "During the twentieth century we have also learned that many new technologies not only sequentially deplete different qualities of resources but also degrade the environment" (Norgaard 1994, 55).

Although coevolution theory is essentially historical in nature, since it cannot definitively predict the various natural or social mutations to come, it can determine some prescriptive remedies for and understandings of obvious problems. Norgaard focuses on "ways of knowing" and "forms of social organization" when discussing the interaction between the environment and the economy. The severe discord between the social subsystems, or the deteriorating coevolution of the universe of man due to environmental and other damage, calls for new "ways of knowing," as well as new social organizations.

> And the emphasis shifts from flows of materials to flows of values, ways of thinking, technologies, ways of organizing people, and natural genetic material. Do not think of these flows, however, as mundane economic exchanges typical of modern trade. . . . If the newly introduced value, way of thinking,

technology, way of organizing, or species prove fit, it will subsequently affect the fitness of other components of the system and thereby change the coevolutionary path of the system, cultural and biological. (Norgaard 1994, 175–76)

The superiority of the economic subsystem over other subsystems needs to be reassessed. The various subsystems cannot be separated, nor can they be ranked in importance. Within the mainstream society this way of thinking may be new, but it is actually a very ancient way of thinking among Native Americans:

> Until I met aboriginals, I had never thought of human beings as participants in a natural system that is endlessly recycled, with every element dependent on every other element. I had always behaved as if society were *perfectible*, had never given thought to life as a natural continuum, in which we also are called upon to act as stewards for future generations. Gradually, I began to understand that all of my assumptions about social progress, personal achievement and human control over the hostile forces of nature are *not necessarily proper measures of a meaningful human existence.* (Richardson 1993, 13; emphasis added)

Boyce Richardson at least recognized that his utility function (in economics parlance) was in need of reformation.

Norgaard provides a framework for understanding social development as complementary to the social compatibility paradigm. Combining Parsonian subsystems with a new understanding of the coevolution of society with the environment provides a rich background for the remainder of this book. Later, I will explain how the history of post-contact policy with respect to Native American peoples led to an obvious downward spiral of their societies. The life situations faced by many, if not most, reservation societies are easily explained by the social theory.

NOTES

1. The only ways into the main village of Supai are by an eight-mile hike, river raft, or helicopter. Even after a devastating flood in 1990, the tribe turned down immediate assistance from students at Northern Arizona University to help with the cleanup. After another flood in 1993, the tribe closed the reservation to all non-members while repairs were made. The discussion concerning the uranium mine occurred before the defense "build-down."

2. Economic Development of the Reservations, Economics 498, senior seminar, fall 1992, Northern Arizona University.

3. Consulting under the auspices of the National Executive Education Program for Native American Leadership (NEEPNAL), Marilyn Enfield was interviewed several times during fieldwork in April, May, and November 1992. At that time Apache Aerospace was planning a major expansion. See Smith and Ozmun 1994.

4. See Cornell and Kalt 1990 for a further discussion of this point.

5. Alternative terms are medicine men, spiritual leaders, and spiritual healers. Navajo culture includes extended ceremonies for a variety of ills and celebrations lasting several days. The singers are the men who oversee and perform these ceremonies.

6. As will be shown, economic development is a likely necessary condition but is by no means sufficient for maintaining cultural integrity.

7. The information concerning Grand Traverse was explained by Chairman Raphael at the 1992 NEEPNAL Tribal Leaders Workshop; the information on Warm Springs comes from White 1990.

8. This quote is attributed to Chief Seattle in 1854 in a speech that he made during treaty negotiations. Jeffers (1991) identifies him as Suquamish, whereas Nabokov (1991, 69), as Duwamish. Wright (1992, 359 n. 55) indicates that the translation of his speech may have been somewhat modified over the years; however, the intent of his speech has not been altered.

9. The introduction of other European technologies such as gunpowder and guns adds to this discussion.

2

Pre-Contact Native American Economic Activity

History books tell the stories. Movies show the scenes. Novels explain the tales. More importantly past and present racism depends on false "facts." And most importantly, past and present federal and state policies are steeped in the ideal. However, the converse is obviously true: Native Americans had extensive and vibrant economic systems of production and trade during the centuries of pre-contact. These systems were as varied as modern-day systems across the globe. Various social, political, and religious structures resulted in great diversity across the Americas. Variations in climate and ecosystems influenced production and trade systems. But the evidence is unequivocal: extensive production occurred side by side with trade activity across the vastness of the Americas.

Healthy and sustainable environmental systems are fully compatible with a prosperous economy. Although there is a vast literature on Native American caretaking, and an equally impressive literature on the extended trade and productions systems of pre-contact Native America, this chapter brings the two together in order to show that sustainable economic systems can work hand in hand with developing cultures. An overview of the interaction between pre-contact economic activity and environmental management illustrates this concord.

One example of an extensive trading network is the Hopewell culture. Jack Weatherford (1991) discusses evidence of a vast economic system within this society. In studying the Hopewell culture, initially identified in present Ohio, in A.D. 400, "we see trade networks that spanned about two-thirds of what is now the United States" (Weatherford 1991, 98). David Thomas (1994, 129–42) indicates that the Hopewell society began to develop around 200 B.C. and quickly became the first pan-Indian religion stretching from "Mississippi to Minnesota, from Nebraska to Virginia" (p. 134). The extensive trading network linking peoples with different languages developed in part to avoid subsistence problems due to local crop or harvest failures. Although localized disasters such as floods or fires might reduce local agricultural output—as well as hunting output—established trade routes would prevent such disasters from resulting in famine. As trade developed, materials other than food were traded. This increased trade resulted in artistic and cultural advances as locally new materials and technologies were adapted to older ones. Thomas concludes that this vast trading network "not only forestalled famine, but also dispersed tons of exotic items across the eastern half of the continent" (p. 139).

The centers of the Hopewell trading network, only minimally based on agriculture, began to diminish around A.D. 500. As the Roman Empire took a dominant position after the Hellenistic period, a new culture and social structure began to replace the Hopewell culture. The Mississippian culture, strongly based on agriculture, had evolved by A.D. 700 and had fully developed by A.D. 850. The political center of the Mississippian was Cahokia.

The evolution or revolution of one "empire" into another follows from the previous discussion of social compatibility, and possibly Richard Norgaard's, theory of social evolution. As agriculture developed and moved into the former Hopewell trading territories, more than just the economic system was changed. The archeological record is far from complete and one hesitates to fictionalize a scenario, but a brief hypothetical scenario raises some interesting possibilities.

As agricultural output increased, possibly through the introduction of corn, less time and effort had to be devoted to food production, and the time saved could have been devoted to the development of the other various subsystems including the polity. Newly advanced characteristics of the polity could have resulted in a more powerful identity for the Mississippian culture. Further advances in the spiritual realm and advances in warfare technology, not uncommonly intertwined, could have resulted in a powerful force.

Historical evidence indicates that most changes from one powerful culture to another typically result from warfare. The developing Mississippian culture was able to overcome the Hopewell communities.

Continuing the hypothetical scenario, I believe that the contraction of the Hopewell communities can be explained by Norgaard's theory. A severe and extended period of drought/rain could have caused an extended period of crop failure. Alternatively, the simplistic agricultural methods of the earlier Hopewell culture may have resulted in depleted productivity.

Combining a declining Hopewell economic and social structure with an advancing Mississippian structure can explain the evolution of social structure. Similar evidence will be provided below concerning the Aztec and Mayan societies. The anthropological evidence concerning the Mississippian culture continues the discussion of pre-contact societies.

Consider the metropolitan area of Cahokia as a second example of extended economic activity.[1] In 1250, this city, located on the Mississippi River in modern Illinois, was larger than London. The estimated 20,000 residents made it one of the world's largest urban centers. Besides the extensive agricultural system and surplus required to support a city of this size, extensive trade existed with other areas. Excavation sites show that this trade network was vast, particularly considering that the only transportation methods were water and foot. Importing copper from the Great Lakes, black chert from Oklahoma and Arkansas, mica from North Carolina, shells from the Gulf of Mexico, salt and lead from Illinois, and stone from Wyoming, "Cahokia united a trading empire larger than the combined area of France, the United Kingdom, Spain, Germany, Austria, Italy, Belgium, the Netherlands, Ireland, Greece, Denmark, Romania, Switzerland, (former) Czechoslovakia, Yugoslavia, Portugal, Luxembourg, and Bulgaria" (Weatherford 1991, 13–14).

The vast trading network could only have supported itself if an intricate economic system was in place. Although no direct evidence of the structure of the system exists, the extent of the network into areas where the cultures are known clearly points to some type of market system. The Cahokia society did not exercise political control over this vast area of trade, so an intricate system of market transactions must have been in place. Many of the listed items could only have been imported through a series of trades as the product took several months or years to travel from the sources to Cahokia. These paths led through the territories of several distinct cultures. Presumably, the mica was shipped from North Carolina by the Cherokees. The mica would have had to travel through, at least, modern Tennessee, Kentucky, and southern Illinois before reaching Cahokia. This trek must have taken months or years and several trades.

Weatherford surmises that Cahokia fell because of the dispersion of European diseases. The diseases advanced at a faster pace than the European explorers and settlers, and the city was deserted by the time Europeans arrived. Clear evidence exists that this phenomenon occurred throughout the Americas. (Indeed, Calvin Martin [1978] bases his hypothesis on it.) Infectious diseases are rampant in any congested urban area, thus providing some validity to Weatherford's argument, although Colin Taylor and William Sturtevant (1991, 15) indicate that Cahokia began to decline in 1250. David Thomas (1994) dates the decline to around 1300, possibly stemming from climatic change. The vastness of the trading network, the comparative size of the urban area, and the extent of the building complexes at Cahokia show clear evidence of a complex economic and social structure regardless of the reason of the community's demise.

The Aztec, Inca, Maya, and Iroquois also show evidence of successful economic systems spanning vast areas of the Americas. As with western European societies and cultures of the same time period, ebbs and flows occurred within the main powers. The Hopewell society declined and was replaced. The Mississippian culture declined and was replaced. The lack of historical information led some to believe that these societies were the victims of some sort of extinction. But new archaeological evidence shows that the process was one of replacement and social evolution. New agricultural techniques possessed by others put the Hopewell society at a relative disadvantage. This major technological change influenced not only the economic structures but also the religious, political, and cultural aspects of the society.

Michael Smith (1997) discusses the historical and archeological evidence from the Aztec Empire. "Yautepec commoners, like their country cousins . . . had ready access to foreign goods. The same kind of imported (goods) . . . were found in residences" (p. 82). "Written sources tell us that Aztec commoners were subjects to nobles, who owned most of the land and monopolized power within the city-states. Archaeological excavations suggest that at least in several provincial settlements, this burden was not excessive" (p. 83).

As with the Hopewell and Mississippian cultures, the Aztec Empire had an extensive trading network. Imported items in provincial villages were as extensive as the ones in the main cities. The polity of the empire was such that the commoners were not highly taxed. Smith argues that the Aztec Empire had a social system that provided a workable compatibility between the social subsystems. The Spanish conquest, as our social theory dictates, led to the demise of the empire.

The evidence of these trading networks is more impressive considering the required interactions between peoples of different cultures and, more importantly, languages. In a moment of extreme racism, Tocqueville ([1835] 1966, 21) wrote: "These American languages seem to be the product of new combinations: those who invented them must have possessed an intellectual drive of which present day Indians hardly seem capable."

Nonetheless, trade took place among peoples with vastly differing languages. The following example shows how this trade might have been accomplished. After Henry Hudson was forced to winter on the shore of James Bay,

A Cree hunter did happen upon Hudson's landfall in the Spring of 1611. Expedition survivor Abacuck Pricket reported that the Cree hunter who arrived at Hudson's camp found himself the centre of much attention. Upon being given a knife, a looking-glass and a handful of buttons, the hunter left, making signs that he would soon return. Showing himself no stranger to the process of trade, he brought back two deer and two beaver skins. Pricket reported the following transaction: "He had a scrip under his arme, out of which hee drew out those things which the Master had given him. Hee took the Knife and laid it upon one of the Beaver skinnes and his Glasses and Buttons upon the other, and so gave them to the Master, who received them and the Savage tooke those things which the Master had given him, and put them in his scrip againe." The bargaining then began in earnest: "then the Master showed him an Hatchet, for which hee would have given the Master one of his Deere skinnes, but our Master would have them both, and so hee had, although not willingly." (Thistle 1986, 3–4)

This example shows several important aspects of the methods of trade. First, Thistle postulates that this was likely the first contact between any Cree and any European; however, the activity of trade was present. Although some European artifacts may have reached this area by 1611, it is highly unlikely that local trade for European items was common. Discussing Samuel Champlain's visits into the interior of modern-day Ontario in 1613, Boyce Richardson (1993) indicates that an inland route to Hudson's Bay had not been found by Europeans. However, such a route was known to the Algonquin's with whom Champlain was negotiating. Thus trade activity, with disparate languages, must have been common among the Cree and other tribes, since it was the hunter who seemingly initiated the trade activity. Second, no time period is given between the hunter's leaving and returning, although Farley Mowat (1989, 88) indicates the Cree returned "after he had slept." Nevertheless, it can be surmised that it was not days or weeks. Therefore the beaver skins show a certain level of "investment" on the hunter's part. Apparently, though an argument can be made otherwise, these skins had already been prepared by the hunter or his family. Whatever other reason the skins were stocked for, the hunter immediately recognized their trade value. Third, a series of relative prices were known or determined by the hunter. Whether or not the goods—knife, looking glass, and buttons—were known to him prior to this meeting, he clearly stipulated a series of prices: one knife for either one beaver skin or one looking glass and the buttons. Fourth, the concepts of variable prices and barter are present in the example. These are all aspects of a complex economic system. Last (and foreshadowing the future), even though Hudson's party was in desperate straits, they took advantage of the hunter.

Thus trade mechanisms were evidently present with pre-contact Native American societies. A second aspect of a productive economy is production technology. The following examples show how production was accomplished.

Weatherford (1991, 103–7) describes the extraordinary architectural knowledge required to build the Mesa Verde community. This knowledge included an understanding of seasonality, solar efficiency, defensive tactics, and agriculture. Weatherford and many others also describe the production of baskets and pottery. The variations in technique show adaptation to local conditions, resources, and needs.

Anthony Aveni (1997) discusses the astronomical *science* of the Mayas. The historical and archeological evidence clearly shows the advanced nature of their astronomical observations and predictions. What use they made of these precise calculations is unknown because of the incompleteness of the extant Mayan written records, but they certainly go beyond the simple procession of the four seasons. Perhaps the astronomical calculations were intertwined with more advanced climatic or environmental cyclic calculations such as El Niño, spiritual occasions, or cycles within the polity. The complexity of the calculations is beyond the power of modern analysis.

An interesting discussion occurred at a conference focused on Indian education at Colorado State University (Mt. Pleasant 1997). Anecdotal discussion included the following comment: "We had our own scientists, engineers, architects, and wildlife managers. Why do we need outsiders to do this for us? We can teach the outsiders about our lands far better than they can teach us." Historical and archeological evidence supports the first idea, and Norgaard's ideas support the latter.

Resource management was also practiced extensively. Perhaps the most useful technique was the use of fire. Controlled fire was used for several different reasons and resulted in many benefits. Although Stewart Holbrook (1943) mistakenly argues that controlled fires did not occur prior to contact, he explains the first benefit of using controlled fires: regularly burning the undergrowth and debris in a forest significantly reduces the harm caused by natural and accidental fires. Controlled fires combined with regular collecting of firewood provided an increased degree of safety when unexpected fires occur.

Several other benefits result from controlled fires (Weatherford 1991, 37–47). Since the controlled fires tend to burn the undergrowth only, mature trees have less competition for nutrients and water. Indeed, the burning replenishes the soil, resulting in straighter and stronger trees: "The European invader regarded these forests as primeval, and their like has not been seen since his steel saws ripped them into boards. But the Cherokees and other Indians had been subtly managing them for thousands of years" (Wright 1992, 98).

Other benefits of fire included better grazing for game animals when the burned undergrowth was replaced by new growth. Furthermore, better grazing meant better hunting not only for humans but also for predators, which coincidentally improved the humans' hunting for predators.

Fire was also used to clear trail systems: "Through the use of fire, Indians maintained large grassy corridors through forests such as those of the Shenandoah Valley, which later served as major migration routes for European settlers" (Weatherford 1991, 43). The trails were also useful in other ways after contact: "When European traders set up in business, they needed only to establish posts on the St. Lawrence, Connecticut, Hudson, and Delaware rivers and Chesapeake Bay to tap into the preexisting native network. Indian traders came to them over preexisting trails on land and by interlaced streams" (Jennings 1992, 363–64). Many of these trails became modern highways.

Pre-contact Native Americans also practiced wildlife management techniques. Unlike forest management, wildlife management involves more than simply taking care of the animals by preventing overhunting. According to Pierre Esprit Radisson, the Cree only harvested adult beavers, leaving the young behind for future hunting. This resource management "could only exist if different groups of Indians respected each other's rights to certain (beaver) lodges" (Bishop 1981, 26), thereby showing a sustainable socioterritorial organization. This facet of the society is vital to understanding the allocation of scarce resources. In order to sustain a viable herd or crop it is essential that the investment be vested to some degree. Further evidence shows that hunting territories were generally respected unless serious shortages were present in neighboring territories. When this happened, neighbors generally allowed "poaching" for subsistence.

This is akin to Thomas's account of the Hopewell culture. Whereas the Hopewell culture maintained trade routes to avoid devastation by famine, northern societies maintained limited property rights for the same reasons. The neighborliness of the social structure provided for vested investment with a potential for sharing in time of need. When situations of need arose, this sharing avoided combat between neighboring families or villages. Again, pre-contact Native communities developed working social structures taking into account the economic system within the context of what the environment allowed.

The other aspect of wildlife management extends the investment approach: "The belief system, I would add, was geared to reinforcing maximum efficiency in subsistence activities so as to avoid 'the wages of poverty'" (Bishop 1981, 53). Arthur Ray extends this idea: "It is clear that native people had developed resource management and redistribution strategies in the pre-contact period which served to minimize the risk of severe privation as a consequence of localized short-term scarcities of basic staples" (1984, 2). (This follows Thomas's discussion of the Hopewell trade networks discussed above.)

Thus the herd management techniques of Native Americans in pre-contact times helped maintain a steady supply of renewable inputs into the production of various goods such as food, clothing, shelter, hunting materials, and the like.

A final type of resource management employed by Native Americans involves agriculture. Tribes in the Southwest (modern Arizona) built extended aqueduct systems well before Columbus, some of which are still used! In addition, an understanding of the natural cycles of the environment based on astronomical and possibly other calculations provided complex systems of crop management. Reporting on the De Soto tour of Choctaw territory, John Bakeless states, "Near each Indian dwelling was a small field (for private use). . . . More distant fields (for communal use), too big to be fenced, were not planted until the wild forest began to ripen, drawing the birds away from new seed" (1950, 53).

Thus the economic system of the Choctaw included an understanding of both the natural environment and shared risk. The small fields required more work to build fences to deter grazing mammals and constant supervision to prevent raiding by birds. These labor-intensive fields were primarily managed by individual families. The larger fields required much less work, involved more risk, and were worked communally. This system is analogous to a modern sole proprietor holding stock in a larger company.

Perhaps the best evidence of the complexity of the economic systems, production technologies, and trade systems present in the pre-contact Americas involves the modern giant of world agriculture: corn, or maize. At the time of Columbus's travels, varieties of corn were grown from Canada to Chile, and from sea level to elevations over 10,000 feet (Warden 1966, 3). The vast differences in climate, soil, growing season, and variety and uses of corn show how complex social interaction in the Americas must have been. Without extensive trade, subtle horticultural knowledge, complex production techniques providing surpluses of other goods while experimentation with corn occurred, and resource management, the distribution of corn could never have occurred. The rationale for such a strong statement is rather simple: agriculturally productive corn—useful corn—is a manmade crop. Howard Warden explains that corn has no way of disbursing its seeds (1966, 6). Any field left unmanaged fails completely within three or four growing seasons. Since the seeds fall so close to the parent plant and are closely grouped in the ears, the subsequent generations choke each other out until the field dies and is taken over by other vegetation. Therefore, corn could not have become so widely dispersed without a system of trade and agricultural management. (Although theft or raids could have dispersed stores, the agricultural knowledge would not have been dispersed.) Furthermore, Jane Mt. Pleasant (1997) indicates the Iroquoian method of growing corn, beans, and squash, while affording an environmentally sound production process, provided "a very comfortable standard of living."

The evidence clearly points to the existence of complex pre-contact Native American societies. Unlike the idealized noble and simplistic savage living in an underutilized paradise, Native Americans developed complex trading networks and production technologies. The supposed lack of technological progress represented a difference in utility functions and resource base. Studies of early settlements show that Europeans were no more suited to live in the American environment than Native Americans were suited to adopt European culture in the ensuing years. The population of the Americas, estimated as possibly 112 million at the time of Columbus,[2] had developed diverse and complex systems for living within their environments.

The idea that these populations were simply hunters, gatherers, and minor farmers is mistaken. When discussing nineteenth-century anthropological methodology, Robert Bieder (1986) describes the work of Albert Gallatin, who believed that Indian culture and production methods were governed by the environment. Gallatin stipulated that the overall environment governed the degree and type of agricultural produce. However, Gallatin and many other writers failed to recognize—as did writers studying European culture—that the culture and social structure also had a strong impact on the environment. Keeping in mind the various resource management techniques described above, it is clear that Native Americans significantly influenced and altered the pre-contact environment. However, unlike the post-contact situation today, their management techniques yielded a healthy and vibrant living place.

This brief survey of pre-contact Native American economies has used archaeological and historical evidence to show the following. Vast trading networks were in place that covered the two continents. These networks involved all the aspects of a modern economic system. Native peoples obviously made investments in capital goods and inventories. Production techniques were complex and relied on the vast trading networks for inputs. Specialization and a division of labor were present. Property rights were well defined for agricultural purposes as well as for harvesting the natural resources. Transportation systems were vast and well developed. In short, pre-contact Native American societies were not primitive subsistence hunting and gathering societies living in simple, naive harmony with the environment. Quite the contrary. These societies managed vast resources within an environmental framework of sustainable development.

NOTES

1. The following is extracted from Weatherford 1991 and Thomas 1994. Many other sources are available for more detailed discussions.

2. See Martin 1978, 44–47. Earlier estimates are lower than more recent estimates. Earlier methods suggest that North America had a population of roughly 1 million. More recent techniques produce larger estimates, which have been confirmed by several methods of estimation. Against a range of 90–112 million for the hemisphere, North America had an estimated population of 9.8–12 million. Of course, the higher the actual population, the stronger the support for the arguments presented in this discussion. Martin seems to agree with the higher estimates.

3

※

Federal Policy Results

The dire poverty and the concomitant social problems facing Native Americans today are a direct result of federal policy, past and present, concerning the indigenous peoples of this country. In this chapter I present a brief overview of these policies and their impact on the cultures under study. A full discussion of these policies is beyond the scope of this chapter—indeed, beyond the scope of a lengthy book.[1] This chapter is merely meant as an appetizer for interested readers, who are referred to U.S. Congress, Senate, Select Committee on Indian Affairs 1989 and Nabokov 1991 for introductions to the history of federal Indian policies. The following discussion relies heavily on these two works for factual information. *The somewhat controversial interpretations in this chapter are solely the responsibility of the author.*

Federal Indian policy has been a complete disaster. From genocide to assimilation to dependency to management, the policies have resulted in unconscionable poverty and social ills. But economic and cultural development is possible under the framework of self-determination policies *if true self-determination is made available to the sovereign nations.*

The federal policy that holds the key to self-determination was the first federal policy: the Constitution defines the Indian Nations as being equal with other foreign nations and states that treaties with the First Nations are to be ratified by the Senate. Therefore, the Constitution of the United States, a document based on the Iroquois form of government between separate "states,"[2] recognizes the sovereignty of Native American tribes. Unfortunately, this ideal did not endure.

The nineteenth century saw the attempted genocide of the indigenous peoples. Military combat combined with intentional germ warfare and unintentional epidemics resulted in a nearly total devastation of the native populations. As the United States expanded westward and then both west and east as the West Coast was developed, the Indian wars proceeded apace.

The reservation system was developed, perhaps because extermination was not a complete success. Tribes were removed from their traditional home sites to locations halfway across the continent or to sites barren, supposedly, of any resources. Hunting and fishing grounds were off-limits or depleted. Treaties were ratified by the Senate only to be renegotiated and ratified again. As a result of this policy, the tribes became completely dependent on federal handouts.

Next came the ideal of assimilation: the Native Americans must be made to fit into American culture. Perhaps this policy came about because it was so very expensive to maintain the reservation populations when most of the expenses went to maintaining the bureaucracy. What follows is a brief interpretational history of the federal policies. Peter Nabokov (1991) provides a detailed testimony of the reactions of Native Americans to these policies.

The Continental Congress and the first U.S. Congress, under the Articles of Confederation, recognized treaties with Indian tribes. The U.S. Constitution stipulates that the Indian tribes are worthy of treaties and that Congress "shall have power . . . to regulate commerce with foreign Nations . . . and with the Indian tribes." Thus it is within the very first policies of the United States that Indian tribes are equal to and comparable with other foreign nations (U.S. Congress, Senate 1989, 27). This policy has been the historical bane of the First Nations. Yet it also holds the key to future development within the context of cultural integrity.

Using the "right of conquest," federal policy aimed at undermining Native America. But recognition of Native sovereignty meant that policy goals treated the First Nations as distinct from immigrant populations. This dichotomy has resulted in convoluted policies and misunderstandings.

Congress enacted several Trade and Intercourse Acts between 1790 and 1834. These acts were aimed at regulating trade across tribal boundaries with the expanding American communities, again recognizing the distinction between the First Nations and the encroaching United States. These Acts also stipulated procedures for acquiring Indian lands as the thirst for expansion continued. At the same time, treaties were signed, which generally followed military conquest.

In 1830, the Indian Removal Act was passed, leading to the Walk of Tears from the eastern states to Indian Country, which became Oklahoma. This was followed by the movement of bureaucratic governance from the Department of War to the Department of the Interior. War occurs between one sovereign nation and another. Thus federal policy was shifting from contracts between sovereign nations to apportioning internal resources. To further this policy, the superintendent system moved the emphasis from governing trade and diplomacy to supervising and managing resources. President Grant's "peace policy" of 1869 aimed at assimilation tactics by proposing schools, churches, and the like for the remaining Indian population. Until this point, federal policy was aimed at controlling the Native American populations to facilitate expansion. Now, a new policy became appropriate. Since expansion was likely to continue until the continent, at least the center part of it between the Rio Grande and the Great Lakes, was governed by the United States, policy shifted from control to assimilation. No longer was it imperative to maintain the peace; rather, conquest and control became the rule of the day, and of the days to follow. No longer could the Indian tribes remain separate from the expanding country: they had to be assimilated into it.

Although arguments have been made considering purely political reasons,[3] the policy of internalizing Indian affairs was viewed as a purely internal problem and resulted in the cessation of treaties making in 1871. However, expressed in an important phraseology for current times, the new policy stipulated that past treaties would be honored

The 1870s and 1880s saw investigations into the results of past Indian policies, which revealed fraud, military errors, bureaucratic ineptitude, inexperienced superintendents, and, inevitably, failures of policy. The Native American population had not only not assimilated but had fallen into outlandish poverty.

Soul searching by congressional leaders led to the Dawes Act of 1887. The General Allotment Act called for doling out parcels of land to individuals, with the surplus lands being sold. Keeping with Grant's policy of assimilation, this policy was supposed to push Native Americans into the capitalistic world. The expanding country required this assimilation.

It should be mentioned, in the current context, that the federal policies mentioned may have been well-intentioned. Federal policy had always aimed at recognizing the rights of the indigenous peoples of the land; however, the political realities involved an expanding population and an ever increasing need for land and resources.[4] The policies aimed at reducing dependency on the federal government during a time of reduced resources for the affected populations. The policies attempted to increase the standard of living of a sector of the overall population that had lost its traditional way of life. The policies also aimed at increasing the level of peace with the encroaching conquering population. However, there was significant discord between policy and practice, as well as rampant fraud and bureaucratic waste. Additionally, unintended results came from a complete misunderstanding of the cultures of Native Americans. The concepts involved with assimilation were cultural anathema to the peoples of the First Nations. Discussing policy in the 1910s, the Senate stated, "As has been the case in the 1890s, however, investigations into social conditions among tribes led legislators to question the administration of federal policies rather than the nature of the policies themselves" (U.S. Congress, Senate 1989, 47).

The intention of the policies, both implicit and explicit, reached a new pinnacle in 1928 when Native Americans were granted U.S. citizenship. Prior to this time, only individuals agreeing to the allotment plan were granted citizenship, regardless of the fact they had volunteered dispro- portionately for service during the First World War.

During the allotment period, 1887–1934, Indian lands were reduced from 136 million acres to 34 million acres. The remainder was sold as "sur- plus." Of the 40 million acres allotted to those eligible, only 17.5 million were in the hands of individual Native Americans (U.S. Congress, Senate 1989, 51). More than 50 percent of the allotted lands had been absorbed by the mainstream economy due to fraud, poverty, or ignorance.

The *Miriam Report* of 1928 diagnosed and documented the fact that assimilation was a nearly complete failure. The results reported earlier were as rampant as ever. Poverty, poor health, lack of education, alcohol abuse, and bureaucratic ineptitude were prevalent in Indian Country.

The federal policy of assimilation had failed. Thus the Indian Reorga- nization Act of 1934 (IRA) was passed. The then Bureau of Indian Affairs (BIA) director, John Collier, began the movement back to recognizing the indigenous peoples as constituting sovereign nations. His policy, however watered down, encapsulates modern hopes for Native American policy. The IRA approved individual constitutions for each of the recognized tribes. Granted, these tended to be "cookie cutter" documents without regard to tribal cultures, and the constitutions were under the auspices of the Secretary of the Interior, this law supplied an opening to self-determi- nation and cultural integrity.

As federal policy oscillated from assimilation and conquest to sover- eign nation, independence gained momentum with the unfolding of the Indian Claims Commission in 1946. This bureaucratic entity was commis- sioned to study and advise on the increasing number of claims concern- ing treaty rights and land and resource issues.

Once the exorbitant costs of these claims started to become apparent, the direction of federal policy once again swung in the other direction. The confusion between well-meaning Indian policy and the expanding country clashed, and expansion won the battle. In 1953, House Concur- rent Resolution 108 and Public Law 280 restricted Indian self-determina- tion. Resolution 108 called for the termination of the Indian Nations, whereas Public Law 280 limited existing tribal control of judicial matters in some states. As a result of these policies, Native Americans were coerced to move from the reservation to urban centers.[5]

With the civil rights movement, the pendulum swung again. The Indian Civil Rights Act of 1968 placed limitations on tribal governments, bring- ing their IRA constitutions in line with the Constitution. Thus began the merging of the past policies. The First Nations were recognized as sovereign nations with the proviso that they were also part of the United States.

In 1970 President Richard Nixon completely restructured federal policy toward Native American sovereignty. The time had come to recognize the First Nations as a viable part of the society as a whole. The results of his suggested policy were two landmark laws. The 1972 Indian Education Act increased parental and community involvement in the educational process of Indian children (gone were the days of enforced boarding schools). The Indian Self-Determination and Education Assistance Act of 1975 provided additional movement toward self-determination by providing for tribes to take over schools from the BIA.

The momentum was building for true recognition of the First Nations as being viable sovereignties. In 1983 President Reagan reformulated the concept of self-determination and stipulated the concept of *self-governance*. Thus federal policy finally recognized the most important reality: the First Nations may have been conquered, but they had not lost their identity. If the United States is to accept this fact, then the Nations first must be recognized as distinct and then must be allowed to make their own decisions. The pendulum has swung back to the first days of the nation: work with the First Nations and not against.

However, Native Americans are still under the auspices of federal policy and its bureaucrats. As is mentioned in the Senate's *Final Report and Legislative Recommendations* (1989, 6), "The federal budget for Indian programs equals $3.3 billion annually. . . . the total household income for American Indians, including the federal government, is actually less than the entire federal budget of $3.3 billion."

Included in income are transfer payments, but excluded from the expenditures are Small Business Administration, welfare, and other payments not depending on the individual or business being Indian. Unfortunately, policy and practice continue to deviate from each other.[6]

Although there is no doubt that the boarding school policy and other policies had a severe impact on native populations and culture in the subsystems of language and religion, these matters lie beyond the scope of this chapter. Similarly, the social consequences of the relocation and termination policies of the 1950s are discussed elsewhere. See Matthiessen 1991 for more detailed discussion of these topics.

For more than two hundred years, federal policy makers have searched for a solution to the "Indian problem." The conflicting goals of resource (land) access and treating Native populations as distinct cultures have brought poverty, poor health, lack of education, alcohol abuse, and bureaucratic ineptitude to Indian Country. Moreover, the federal investigations of the 1980s revealed circumstances very similar to those documented by 1880s investigations and the *Miriam Report*. After two centuries of searching for solutions, federal policy has reverted to the first policy: self-determination.

Perhaps the best example of the conflict between control and self-determination dictates is that of Indian gaming. The continuing imbalance between self-control and governance has resulted in a very confusing set of regulations and compacts among federal, state, and tribal governments. Regardless of this confusion, Indian gaming has resulted in extraordinary success for some tribes.

However, there are still concerns over resources owned by the Native American Tribes. BIA management of tribal assets is still prevalent, either by the BIA directly or through previously negotiated contracts with resource extraction companies. But movement is under way for tribes to take control of these resources and manage their own decisions. The White Mountain Apache Tribe has taken over control of timber processing operation under the 638 legislation.[7] This involved developing a complete management system prior to the formal takeover. Both the Navajo and Hopi Tribes are attempting to renegotiate the BIA-negotiated contract with Peabody Coal in light of the exorbitant use of water from the aquifer. Other tribes are attempting to develop their own resources, the BIA notwithstanding.

In the words of one tribal planner, the BIA has gone from a stance of deterrence to one of ambivalence. Of course, he hopes the BIA will go one step further (Goforth 1992)! In short, federal policy has begun to aim at developing the resources on Indian lands for the benefit of the Native population. Thus the two conflicting goals of past policies have merged into a rather simple and seemingly obvious policy: allowing the tribes to develop their own resources makes resources available to the mainstream economy at market prices, and the profits and benefits of this development go to the owners of those resources. In the long run this policy will reduce Native American dependency on federal programs, the resources being made available to non-Indians, and, potentially, will maintain and develop the cultures of the First Nations. The path to development, therefore, lies in realizing the concept of self-determination.

The form of the resulting government needs to be compatible with the rest of the social system. However, this has not been the case. Besides the linkages between culture and economic activity, Philip Corrigan and Derek Sayer (1985) identify the linkages between culture and the government or state:

> States, if the pun be forgiven, state; the arcane rituals of a court of law . . .
> They define, in great detail, acceptable forms and images of social activity
> and individual and collective identity; they regulate, in empirically specifi-
> able ways, much—very much by the twentieth century—of social life. (p. 3)

This statement is even more important because most, if not all, of federal regulations concerning Native Americans have been formulated without any input from them. The separation between the economy and the polity is important in that Native Americans have had little input into the discussions of making compatible decisions between the subsystems of their societies. Both in terms of resources allocation and income distribution—the engines of social progress—Native Americans have had to accept allocations and regulations clashing with the remainder of their aboriginal cultures—even when those cultures evolved to approximate acceptable levels of compatibility. Given the conditions on most reservations, compatibility involving sustainability and self-sufficiency has not occurred.[8]

The recurring incompatibility results from two important conflicts. The first conflict involves two disparate goals formulated by the dominant society, goals that could never be simultaneously fulfilled. The second conflict arises from diverse forms of incompatibility between one of those federal goals and the existing social systems of the aboriginal societies when the policies went into effect. In this section I briefly discuss the conflicts inherent in past federal policy toward the Indian tribes.

Federal policy has had two competing policy goals when dealing with the First Nations: recognition of sovereignty and resource acquisition. The first policy goal acknowledges the Indian Nations as individual and sovereign entities with which treaties and international agreements are to be made. The second policy, best defined by the doctrine of Manifest Destiny, includes acquiring all available resources for use and employment in the economy of the United States. Given that these two goals are diametrically opposed, it is little wonder that federal Indian policy continues to result in dire consequences for those living under such policies.

The Indian Nations have been identified as equal to other nations in the Trade and Intercourse Acts of 1790–1834, the IRA legislation and resulting tribal constitutions, the Indian Claims Commission, the Indian Civil Rights Act of 1968, the Indian Education Act of 1972, and the Indian Self-Determination and Education Assistance Act of 1975, among others. The Reagan administration included self-governance as a policy aim. To some extent, the reservation system also fits into the sovereignty goal (discussed below).

These policies had the goal of recognizing the Indian Nations as identifiable, self-governing, and sovereign from the powers of the United States. Unfortunately conflicting with the policy goal of resource acquisition, they produced results that fell well short of their aim.

The policies derived from the second goal included extermination, as best defined by Governor Pitkin of Colorado following conflicts with the Utes:

> My idea is that, unless removed by the government, they must necessarily be exterminated. I could raise 25,000 men to protect the settlers in twenty-four hours. The state would be willing to settle the Indian trouble at its own expense. The advantages that would accrue from the throwing open of 12,000,000 acres of land to miners and settlers would more than compensate all the expenses incurred. (As quoted in Brown 1970, 388)

Fortunately (or unfortunately, depending on your position), these policies failed due to the extreme cost of fighting wars against enemies unfamiliar with European battle tactics. The Indian Wars were very expensive, especially when combined with the aftermath of the Civil War.[9] One estimate of the campaign expenses for the Powder River expedition of 1865 was that: "at an expense of more than a million dollars [per dead Indian], while hundreds of our soldiers had lost their lives, many of our border settlers been [sic] butchered, and much property destroyed" the campaign had basically failed (Brown 1970, 123). Other resource acquisition policies included shifting responsibility for the "Indian problem" from the Department of War to the Department of the Interior. War occurs between one sovereign nation and another, whereas the new designation called for managing resources. Assimilation policies, such as Grant's "peace policy," aimed at simply merging the Indian population with the rest of the country. The Dawes Act, or General Allotment Act of 1887, was similarly planned, as were the boarding schools, in the House Concurrent Resolution 108 calling for the termination of the Indian Nations and Public Law 280 limiting tribal jurisdiction. All of these policies were aimed at the opposite result of the sovereignty policies: reducing the Indian population to, at best, be part of the population as a whole. As discussed above, various parts of the Indian societies could not be industrialized into a capitalistic framework and, therefore, the policies failed.

The conflict between these two goals resulted in several very incompatible policies. The first of these was the Indian Removal Act of 1830. In order to meet both goals, the five sovereign "civilized" nations were forcibly marched across the continent. The sovereignty of the nations was protected and a vast resource was vacated. The reservation system is really a perversity exacerbated mismanagement. Somehow, the conflicting federal goals concerning the Indian problem converged into a policy that isolated the so-called sovereign nations on supposedly resource-poor land bases that were then managed by the federal government. Obviously, a societal structure evolving in the environment of one set of resources, say central Florida or the Blue Ridge Mountains, would not necessarily be compatible with a completely different set of resources, say Oklahoma. Combining this with the fact that the new polity and economy of the nations clashed with the other subsystems of the indigenous cultures, it is hardly surprising the policies resulted in the dire consequences seen on reservations to this day. Discussing the policy of the 1910s, the Select Committee on Indian Affairs stated, "As has been the case in the 1890s, however, investigations into social conditions among tribes led legislators to question the administration of federal policies rather than the nature of the policies themselves" (p. 47).

Considering that the policies stemmed from two very contradictory goals, it is little wonder the policies, let alone the administration thereof, failed. The same Select Committee reached similar conclusions concerning the policies of the 1980s.

Stephen Cornell and Joseph Kalt (1991) point out a further conflict inherent in recent times. It can be argued, from a bureaucratic theory perspective, that the goal of the BIA is to maintain poor living standards on the reservations in order to maximize its budget.

Federal policy has vascillated between these two conflicting goals. Not only do these goals conflict with each other, they also clash with the cultures of many of the people they aim at regulating. By treating the indigenous cultures as nation-states, the policies aimed at sovereignty frequently clashed with those cultures. Thus in many cases, the seemingly agreeable goal of recognizing sovereignty was (and is) incompatible with the remaining aspects of the indigenous cultures.

The Constitution of the United States is heavily based on a Native American form of government. The Iroquois had a stable governmental structure that attracted the interest of Benjamin Franklin and others.[10] However, for many tribes, the concept of a central government was (and is) not part of the shared property of the society. Federal policy forced the First Nations to become just that: nations. The nations were defined by federal regulation and restriction in conjunction with the underlying cultures. These definitions, regulations, and restrictions conflict with traditional polity issues on several levels.

Although some aboriginal societies had well-formed governmental structures matching those of the enforced ones, many of the so-called Indian nations did not. Following the above discussions of Talcott Parsons, and Corrigan and Sayer, it follows that interactions between government and culture reach an equilibrium; therefore, it is folly to conclude that the First Nations societies did not have governmental structures. Students of anthropology and history are well aware of this. As noted in chapter 2, the social, political, and economic systems were very well developed. However, the structure of governments (States state) was compatible with the remaining subsystems of the societies. Policies that forced Indians to adopt other governmental structures threw these societies into a predicament of incompatibility.

The obvious example of this is when two or more distinct societies were thrown together under a single tribal designation. For example, the Warm Springs Reservation includes portions of three distinct aboriginal societies. Forcing these societies to live under one set of rules and ignoring past conflicts create conflict within the resulting societal systems.

Another example is when the new governmental structure is incompatible with traditional structure. The classic example is the Hopi Tribe. The traditional system was based on "city-states" in which each community reached a consensus; when appropriate, the collection of individual communities then reached a consensus. Placing a majority rule central government in power, federal policy aggravated dissension among the modern Hopi.

A third example of the conflict between imposed government and traditional government is best exemplified by comparing the Sioux Reservations and the Apache Reservations. Traditional Apache government focused on community needs and was directed by a strong leader. As with the Iroquois Nations, this leader stayed only as long as the population agreed with his decisions. Alternatively, traditional Sioux Communities were more concerned with local issues. Similar to traditional Hopis, the Sioux did not have a strong central government. Traditionally, the Sioux were very individualistic. Unlike the Hopi, who required consensus, Sioux individuals, families, and clans could decide to go against the decision of the majority. Subjecting this sociological structure to democratic majority rule in a central government model results in continual turmoil.

Thus, the sovereignty that federal policy goals promoted among Indian tribes was designed by the dominant society. In this case, a strong central government caused less incompatibility for the Apache than for the Sioux tribes. Combined with the above mentioned aggregation of disparate groups, federal policy concerning the Sioux simply did not mesh with traditional governmental structures.

Cornell and Kalt (1992a) conclude that tribes with current governmental structures similar to traditional structures are far more likely to be economically successful. Apache societies traditionally were led by strong central leaders. These communities worked well with a strong central government, and the Apache economies were successful compared to the Sioux economies, for two reasons. The imposed structure caused less disruption to traditional methods of decision making, and the traditional methods were more compatibly merged with an industrial capitalistic economic system. This does not imply assimilation; rather, the enforced policies were less influential on other aspects of the society.

Assimilation does not usually work with Native Americans. Nor does it work with many other ethnic groups: the American reality and strength is a diversity of culture and belief and society. The time has finally come to accept and allow Native American cultures to develop and succeed. After all, the very structure of the Constitution is based on a Native American model. Further evidence of the need for practical solutions to the continuing "Indian problem" is the recognizing that the tribes are still unlikely to give up their fight for sovereignty and individuality. Consider the results when push came to shove at Wounded Knee in 1973,[11] Oka, Quebec, in 1990,[12] and St. Regis in 1997.

Past and current federal policy toward the Native populations has had serious conflicts with the Native social structures. Intentionally or not, these policies have caused a drastic downward spiral in the social systems of reservation communities.

The recent policy of self-determination, barely twenty-five years old, follows centuries of conflict among the social subsystems. The potential for this new policy has to be understood as what it is: a path toward success without any guarantee. Given the current status of the remaining subsystems, a newly reconstituted polity can only evolve if the remaining subsystems are also modified to reach higher levels of compatibility.

NOTES

1. For instance, see the 3119-page, four-volume collection by Wilcomb Washburn (1973).

2. See Wright 1992, 116 for an expanded discussion of this point. The Iroquois constitute a league of separate nations. Originally there were five tribes in the confederacy, which expanded to six tribes in post-Columbian times.

3. The House of Representatives, concerned about its lack of power vis-à-vis the Senate, took some power from the Senate (U.S. Congress, Senate 1989, 41).

4. Compare the described policies with those of the conquest of Africa, specifically, past South African policies.

5. My own family experienced Canada's similar attempt. In 1931–32, the Canadian government offered $50 per head to any Indian moving off the reservation (or so goes family lore), an exorbitant amount of money for a destitute Depression-era family. Interestingly enough, this procedure was called enfranchisement. By giving up all rights as Mohawks, the family became enfranchised into Canadian society. Recent legislation allows for enfranchised Indians and their progeny to regain their Native rights.

6. In this chapter I do not describe in detail the inefficiency of the BIA and all other Indian policies. Rather, I focus on positive avenues of development regardless of the federal bureaucracy. See U.S. Congress, Senate 1989; Presidential Commission on Indian Reservation Economics 1984; and U.S. Department of the Interior 1986 for details. Also, see many other sources detailing the idiocy of the federal bureaucratic infrastructure. As this book goes to press, additional reports are detailing the complete disaster of accountability by the federal government regarding trust accounts.

7. See Krepps 1991 for a discussion of the 638 results in the timber industry. His conclusions show that tribally run timber enterprises are significantly more profitable than BIA-managed enterprises.

8. Other disruptions such as boarding schools and religion suppression are beyond scope of the current discussion. The focus of this book is on the importance of developing the economic system.

9. See Churchill 1997 for a detailed discussion of these issues.

10. See Wright 1992, 116 for an expanded discussion of this point.

11. See Matthiessen 1991.

12. See Wright 1992, 331–42.

4

A Paradigm for
Economic Development

The previous chapters have provided a background for understanding the importance of economic development within reservation communities.[1] This chapter establishes a paradigm for accomplishing economic development within a social compatibility context. Chapters 5–6 extend the discussion by focusing on the interaction between an economic system and cultural integrity.

Economic development is the engine for overall social development. As Native America becomes integrated into the global economy, decisions have to be made regarding economic activity such that a cohesive structure develops within a cultural context.

In an article entitled "Native American Economic Development: A Modern Approach" (Smith 1994a) I explained a conceptual framework of economic development for Native American reservations. Invoking a model first developed by Jane Jacobs (1984), I provided a theoretical framework for understanding regional development.[2] For sustained economic growth I suggest a four-stage cycle. This chapter briefly discusses the background ideas of the development cycle in the context of reservation economies.

The first stage of the cycle of growth involves an initial export industry earning imports. At first glance it might be said that an economy facing over 50 percent unemployment and concomitant dire poverty does not have many such export industries; however, reservation economies clearly have the ability to import products. Tribes do earn revenues from extractive enterprises such as mines, forestry projects, and water sales. Other tribal and private enterprises provide some degree of earnings. A

45

variety of federal, state, and tribal government activities provide additional employment. Besides these salaries, royalties, and profits earned from tribal activities, other major sources of funds are transfer payments and trust account earnings. Recently, many tribes have begun to earn imports with the profits from their gaming facilities. In a few cases, these profits are substantial. Therefore most tribes do satisfy the requirement of earning imports. Moreover, private imports are typically purchased from the border towns on day trips by residents spending transfer and other income. Thus the first stage of the cycle is satisfied.

The second stage, which is of primary importance in the current context, is the development of import-replacing industries within the local economy. In this stage, the reservation economy begins to produce locally hitherto imported products. The import-replacing phase allows for a drastic reduction of the leakages to border communities. In terms of reservation economies, this primarily means an increase in retail and service activity. An extension of this idea is the actual production of some of the products previously imported.

The import-replacement phase does *not* reject the tenet of comparative advantage; rather, it expands on the understanding that trade patterns should follow well-known economic fundamentals. The forcefulness of the import-replacing idea rests on the understanding that comparative advantages are not static in nature.[3] By reducing transport distances and developing new and improved technology—not to mention lower wage rates on the reservation—a tribe may well be able to import replace some previously imported products at a cost savings. For example, relatively low wage rates on the reservations make conducting business there more profitable. Since wages rates averaged $4.10 per hour in the nations of Hong Kong, Korea, Singapore, and Taiwan in 1992 (Pomice and Hawkins 1992), there is a competitive advantage for reservations when transportation costs are factored in. Thus the potential for developing manufacturing and assembly work is significant. Additionally, several federal programs aimed at advancing minority-owned businesses present opportunities for tribally owned and privately owned businesses. The problem is to identify products that can be successfully produced by the tribe, which of course is the question any development plan must answer. Regional science analysis has produced various techniques to help determine the sectors and industries potentially ripe for expansion, but these problems are beyond the scope of the current discussion. Clearly, the activities to be import replaced are reservation specific, but once the products and services are identified and the tribe begins to domestically produce the product, it is then possible that the direction of the comparative advantage actually reverses through the process, which is the next stage in the cycle.

The third stage involves developing new and innovative products and production techniques during the import-replacing phase. For example, modern Navajo arts and crafts industries include world-renowned techniques for weaving and silversmithing. Techniques for dying and spinning wool have progressed from rudimentary ones to advanced techniques allowing for intricate designs and patterns. Originally, Navajos developed these industries for domestic consumption of jewelry and blankets; however, these industries are now significant sources of income for individual artisans and the tribally managed Navajo Arts and Crafts Enterprise.

The fourth stage encompasses developing these new techniques and products into new export industries, which provide increased or substitute import-earning income. At this stage, the process cycles: new import-replacing takes place, which develops new products, which cultivates a new phase of exports. Thus a cycle of vigorous growth obtains.

APPLYING THE MODEL

In order to identify those industries available for import-replacing and export development, it is necessary for the local economy to have an understanding of its resource base. For instance, the San Carlos Apache Tribe may feel that semiconductor manufacturing is a reasonable industry to enter, either as a sole or a joint venture. Such a venture will require the availability of employees with engineering and management skills. As discussed below, a labor survey may point out a shortage of engineering skills within the local population, making such a venture infeasible. However, it may be discovered that range and herd management skills are available at surplus levels. Thus expanding the tribal cattle enterprise may be more feasible than retraining the population. Then a long-term import-replacement goal of meat packing may be envisioned, which will allow the necessary time to educate students in the management and science skills necessary for such an operation. Further study will help explain the process.

Consider the following, for example. The White Mountain Apache Tribe in Arizona has a small manufacturing facility producing parts for the Apache helicopter produced by McDonnell-Douglas. After five years of operation, the tribe expanded its operations from simple "cut-and-sew" operations to more advanced production. The planned expansion of Apache Aerospace involved diversified products and an increased marketability to aerospace companies besides McDonnell-Douglas. The new technology utilized included the Mentor-Protégé legislation.[4] Marylin Enfield vigorously lobbied for the passage of this legislation (Enfield 1992).

Jane Jacobs best describes the process of sustained development:

> Any settlement that becomes good at import replacing *becomes* a city. And any city that repeatedly experiences, from time to time, explosive episodes of import replacing keeps its economy up-to-date and helps keep itself capable of casting forth streams of innovative work. Why "explosive" and why

"episodes"? In real life, whenever import replacing occurs significantly at all, it occurs in explosive episodes because it works as a chain reaction. The process feeds itself, and once well under way, does not die down in a given city until all imports that are economically feasible to replace at that time and in that place have been replaced. (1984, 41)

Jacobs states that *any* "settlement" can become involved with the development process, and I vigorously believe that this process can be applied to reservation economies. Jacobs argues that what makes a "city region" a cohesive entity is a central identity. Nowhere is this identity more pronounced than on and near reservations. Jacobs also argues—as do other regional analysts—that political borders are unimportant in the development process, except for defining sovereignty, legal and tax systems, and their impacts. Keeping with that thought, what makes a reservation and its border towns a cohesive whole is the cultural and economic linkages existing within a definable region with a definable population. The development cycle begins with no precondition other than an initial earnings of imports, which currently occurs within reservation economies. She also explains growth and development as a process, not a static burst of energy. Thus the "explosive episodes" in Indian Country will start small and grow over time. The initial episode will likely evolve over the next fifteen to twenty years. This follows some five hundred years of stagnation and deterioration.

Growth occurs from the import-replacing and export-development process because of five interwoven considerations. First, as import replacing occurs, a growing number and diversity of employment opportunities develop. Second, as employment earnings increase and the multiplier effect obtains, the region has enlarged import markets providing imports of new and different kinds. Third, as activity and employment increase, jobs and activity spread outward from the city hub to the hinterlands, thereby increasing economic activity in the surrounding areas. Fourth, as the process continues, there will be new uses for existing technology and new technological developments as entrepreneurial activity occurs. And last, as the process proceeds and new businesses are opened, there will be an increase in the capital stock of the city region. These five forces of growth lead to increased economic activity and employment and toward the development of the cycling of growth: new exports earning increased and new imports. And the process cycles.

Tribal concerns for developing master plans for development reflect their understanding that progress is required to take them from their current situation to a position of self-determination and self-sufficiency. Barbara Ward describes the need for an overall plan of action as follows:

All parts of the economy have to be affected if the economic pattern as a whole is to change. A little modification here, a little development there, may transform parts of the economy, but it is only when the flood of change begins to run right through society that you get that actual "breakthrough" to a new type of productive economy. (1962, 34)

Understanding that development is a process governing the entire economy and that the entire economy must take part in the progress is vital. Furthermore, the model does not simply apply to existing city centers; rather, it applies to any cohesive society striving for development (i.e., it is a relevant model for reservation strategies).

While our model is segmented into individual phases, it does so because of the necessity for narrative simplicity. In a practical sense, the cycle is an ever changing motif of phases for different industries and sectors. As such, the individual parts of the whole need not be mutually exclusive. Import replacing of one product can occur side by side with export development of another service. Also, export development need not be a direct result of import replacement; rather, some exports may result as a sole effort to increase import earning potential without any intention of local consumption. For example, consider White Mountain Apache's success in producing component parts for the Apache helicopter. Other than for demonstration purposes, none of the final product (combat helicopters) is of any use to this tribe.

Jacobs initially uses the term city to identify an economic aggregation of activity in which the bulk of economic activity is based on interactions within that region. In many cases, the centering node for this activity is an identifiable city. However, she uses examples focusing on national regions and small town regions. She further explains supply regions and transplant regions. Therefore, her model of a "vigorous city" should not be limited to large city centers; rather, the idea that a region has a cohesiveness is essential to our current discussion. Reservation economies, particularly geographically isolated ones, have all the characteristics of a connected region as mentioned above. Furthermore, many off-reservation border towns are part of the reservation economy, and not the other way around. One of the goals of import replacing retail and service industries onto the reservation is to tighten the economic ties within the reservation and limit those with off-reservation businesses. Jacobs describes the process of development as defining a vigorous city and does not require the existence of a certain population size or density.

Considering development models, two important aspects are required for local reservation development. First, import replacement takes advantage of the multiplier effect. According to one study, 87 percent of disposable income of the Navajo Nation is spent off the reservation (Yazzie 1989).

The multiplier effect is straightforward. If 87 percent of all dollars arriving instantly go to the border towns, then only 13 percent is spent on the reservation. Of a single dollar, 87 percent of the thirteen cents leaves the reservation and so on. The total effect of that single dollar is

$1.15. If the situation is turned around such that 87 percent of every dollar of income is spent on the reservation, then the single dollar creates up to $7.69 of additional spending. This simplified example assumes that all of the on-reservation spending results in on-reservation income. If the store is owned by a nonreservation entity, then the profits leak as well. If the product being sold is imported, then the multiplier is weakened.

If reservations are to develop, leakages to border towns must be diminished. Fully understanding the multiplier effect, President John Yellow Bird Steele of the Oglala Sioux Tribe states, "Spending that dollar in our jurisdiction—at least once if not more than once" is an important goal (Steele 1992). As mentioned previously, import replacing retail and service industries onto the reservation will stimulate economic activity. In a very real sense, trade deficits between the reservation and the mainstream economy limit the effects of the multiplier effect. Counterbalancing the importance of domestic production are the benefits of trade due to comparative advantage. Keeping earned surpluses revolving within the local economy enhances employment and incomes within that economy. Either an economy must increase its domestic trade through the multiplier effects or it must increase its exports to earn increased imports. Import replacing and increased domestic production do not work against export development; rather, the sectors work in conjunction and enhance each other.

Second, increasing the economic viability of these economies requires developing export enterprises: without interaction with the global economy, reservations are facing isolation leading to continued subservience. Exports earn income for the domestic economy. These increased earnings can be used to purchase increased imports or filtered through the domestic economy with added influences of the multiplier effect. The benefits of trade due to comparative advantages need to be balanced with the secondary and tertiary effects of domestic economic activity.

Therefore, most tribes need to form a two-pronged attack in their economic development plans. A mixture of import replacing, increasing the effects of the multiplier effect, and increased export development, earning increased incomes, accelerates the multiplier mechanism. Combining this with a meaningful and purposeful increase in imports will allow the reservation economies to improve their self-sufficiency and economic freedom. Besides the multiplier effects and the increased employment opportunities leading to higher standards of living, there will also be a reduced reliance on government employment. President Steele mentions the problems with relying on government employment due to the scarcity of other opportunities: "people are interested in federal service jobs and not the goals, services and roles of those jobs" (Steele 1992).

At this point, a clarification is necessary. The development paradigm recognizes the importance of import replacing; however, the aim of economic development is to develop new or at least increased exports, thereby raising income and earning increased imports. In general, the end implies the middle, but this need not be the case.[5] Take, for instance, the Yavapai–Prescott Reservation. This small reservation currently runs a successful gaming operation and leases land to ITT for a Sheraton conference center. Neither of these two enterprises is aimed at import replacement; rather, this tribe jumped straight to the export development phase. The tribe has also developed a shopping center that includes a Wal-Mart store and a supermarket. Again, this facility serves the city of Prescott and not just the reservation population. Besides rents and revenues from the gaming operation, the tribe assesses a privilege charge equal to the state sales tax. Thus the tribe is able to earn increased imports—has increased income—without benefits of the multiplier effect or import replacing. This example does not diminish, however, the general importance of the import replacement phase as an important step in the development process. Very small tribes, bands, and especially gaming tribes located near a city may be able to develop by attracting the border town to reservation activities; larger tribes probably need to develop their own economic infrastructure.

Similar to skipping a step in the model, reservation economies also have the ability to "leapfrog technologies." José Goldemberg and Hal Harvey (1997) explain how developing economies are able to "skip some of the earlier, dirtier stages of industrial development and instead go straight to the more advanced, cleaner technologies." Although their focus is on environmental issues, the implication is also applicable to the model. One of the benefits of import replacing and the development of new exports is the opportunity to improve on the technologies used in the border towns. A possible example would be a communications company using digital technology.

THE CONCEPT OF AN ECONOMIC BASE

Charles Tiebout introduces his seminal work, which still serves as the source work for designing economic base studies, with the following paragraph:

> The economic base of a community consists of those activities which provide the basic employment and income on which the rest of the local economy depends. An economic base study identifies the basic sources or employment and income in a community. The primary objective of an economic base study is to develop information which will help a community solve local problems, make better decisions about matters that will enlarge economic opportunities for its citizens, improve their welfare, and make it possible for them to increase their contributions to national growth. (1962, 9)

With the possible exception of the last goal, reservations have the same list of goals. Although more advanced techniques have been developed since Tiebout's landmark work, the framework remains the same, and a simple economic inventory of a reservation's existing and potential assets can prove helpful. This section presents a discussion of how the classic economic base study can be adapted to provide helpful information to a tribal government about the potential areas for development.

Whereas the model provides a paradigm for development activities, it does not immediately lead to a list of suggestions in terms of specific development projects. In order to identify the industries and services most likely to be profitable for import replacement and export expansion, the tribal government must have an understanding of the available and potential resources. Additionally, the analysis can identify areas in which resources must be developed.

H. Craig Davis begins his exposition on economic impact analysis with the following:

> Individual citizens, businesses, community, and commercial organizations, as well as government agencies at various levels, have long been interested in the nature and magnitude of local economic changes that result from a variety of public and private sector initiatives. (1990, 3)

The primary data necessary for an economic base study include an inventory of existing economic activity showing the interactions between various activities within the local economy. Using these preliminary data, the analyst is able to model a structure of the local economy and is then able to analyze the consequences of planned or future events, depending on the complexity of the model used. The required data include a listing of existing business enterprises and government agencies, along with their employment skills and labor requirements. More advanced analysis includes levels and types of capital, capital funding availability, and other input requirements.

Concerning the design of data collection and primary investigation, Davis (1990) explains that when "the economic transactions within the region are sufficiently complex to preclude judgment or an ad hoc approach, the analyst must turn to other means. An obvious alternative or complement to judgment is to survey the various establishments in the region to ascertain the total employment of each and the division of sales to markets within and outside the region" (p. 15).

The local economies of Native American reservations are sufficiently complex, with a severe lack of data availability, to preclude making short- or long-term plans using simple ad hoc analysis. Furthermore, the concerns of Native American reservations are significantly different from those requiring the classic economic base analysis to warrant pivotal changes in the analysis methodology.

The economic structures of Native American reservations differ considerably from nonreservation economies of similar population or land area. First, most reservations face exorbitantly high rates of unemployment.

Furthermore, much of the employment available on reservations involves governmental work of some sort. For example, the Hualapai Nation had an employment structure in which 45 percent of the working population were government employees, and the Fort Mohave Reservation had a combined government employment of rate 75 percent (Arizona Department of Commerce 1990).[6] Combining these facts with low educational achievement makes economic development difficult. Other factors deterring development include sovereignty issues facing tribes and the trust nature of most of the land available to the tribes. Additionally, many businesses located on reservations are enterprises directly or indirectly controlled by the tribal government. Thus many economic development plans entail initiating a tribal enterprise either as a freestanding business or as a joint venture with an off-reservation corporation. The aim of the development plans is to increase the utilization levels of the drastically underutilized resources available to the tribes.

Thus questions concerning economic expansion must be restated in a format that makes sense in a Native American cultural and a reservation framework. In developing a long-term strategic plan, the tribal government needs to know what resources are available for development. In terms of natural resources, most tribes know those located on the reservation because of past, and current, exploitation plans of the tribe, the BIA, or other outside agents. Alternatively, few tribes fully understand their labor resources. The questions concerning the existing labor force are threefold. First, what resources are available for development? Second, what activities should be avoided due to current deficiencies in the labor force? Third, which of these deficiencies can be diminished through future training and education programs?

The first question can be answered with a detailed inventory of the existing population. A population survey is required, as opposed to the existing employment force detailed by Davis, because the tribe is interested in knowing the characteristics of the surplus of available labor as well as the existing labor force. Using this information will enable the tribe to formulate a plan of action utilizing those skills.

Consider, for example, the following scenarios. The labor survey shows a tribe to have a significant number of unemployed, underemployed, or discouraged individuals with skills in both child care and basketry. The individuals with child care skills are unemployed due to a lack of demand for their services, whereas the individuals skilled in basketry are underemployed or discouraged due to their child care responsibilities. To this imaginary scenario add several underemployed individuals with marketing and management skills. Having gained this information from a labor skills survey, the tribe might form a cooperative enterprise for tribal members skilled in basketry, managed and marketed by tribal members. Meanwhile, the tribal members skilled in child care can open a child care service. This would facilitate the operation of the coop and other enterprises.

Another example would involve an underemployed individual with an M.B.A., an electrical engineering graduate, and twenty unemployed high school graduates with a variety of skills. In this case, the tribe could search for a joint-venture project producing parts for some electrical machinery, such as circuit boards or electrical harnesses. Both of these enterprises hold the opportunity to employ twenty or more tribal members, with the potential for the employment multiplier adding to the impact of the enterprises.

The possibility of deficiencies within the existing population is also an important consideration of the labor skills survey. Suppose the tribe is negotiating, or is approached to do so, with a firm requiring the same electrical harnesses mentioned above. However, an analysis of the labor skills survey shows that the skills required for this production are not available. This recognition will avoid the difficulties of entering into a contract that cannot be completed, thus avoiding the possible loss of investment capital, employment, and goodwill. For example, in its early years, Apache Aerospace entered into a contract with the U.S. Navy; however, there was no possibility Apache Aerospace could meet the requirements of the contract without absorbing exorbitant loses (Enfield 1992).

Given limited resources and the communal nature of many tribal decisions, tribes need to allocate their education funds in a manner that best fits their future needs. The following example provides insight to this requirement for a labor skills survey. A manufacturing firm anticipates an expansion from 20 to approximately 150 employees. Besides production workers, the enterprise needs an accounting expert and an engineering supervisor. The production workers need a certain level of fundamental education and job-specific skills. Through the Job Training Partnership Act funds, the tribe may have the possibility of training programs; however, these funds are limited. The labor skills survey will allow the tribe to identify those individuals best qualified for employment and training. Without the labor skills survey the enterprise will have to use an ad hoc basis for identifying individuals for training, which may result in a shortage of funds and a shortage of employable individuals. Currently, without training, the enterprise faces a deficiency of employable tribal members; however, understanding the available labor pool assets and the deficiencies allows them to formulate training and production plans. Additionally, the need for an accounting and an engineering specialist focuses a current deficiency within the tribal membership. However, scholarship plans and awards can be designed to fill this void in the future by tying scholarship funds to these specific fields of study.

In short, for a tribe to fully understand its economic base and the potentials for economic development, it must understand the available resources. Currently, the primary void in data availability concerns the population's labor skills inventory. Once the survey is completed, the tribe will be able to plan specific goals and objectives. Using the inventory data, an inventory of other available resources, and an understanding of the development process, the tribe will be able to formulate a long-term strategic plan for the future.

Thus the economic base analysis for reservations must include a different type of analysis than that used for more active communities. Rather than study the existing economy, the reservation-based study has to include an analysis of the unemployed and underemployed resources. Fortunately, much of the required information is readily available: natural resource inventories, tribal enterprise profit and income histories, tribal expenditures on imported and domestically produced goods and services, infrastructure descriptions and utilization rates, housing occupancy and characteristics. The main lack of information involves data concerning individual tribal members employment potentials and expenditure habits.

A HYPOTHETICAL EXAMPLE

It is important for a tribal government to understand the employability of its members. There are many instances in which a detailed employable skills inventory and assessment may come in handy.

For instance, many tribal governments are approached regarding possible joint ventures with outside businesses. Imagine the following scenario. A reputable national firm interested in locating an assembly plant on the reservation approaches a tribal government. The national firm is interested in a reservation site for both financial and social reasons. They feel that a joint project will be financially advantageous due to the tax and wage considerations associated with a reservation location. The tribe will own the plant, but initially the national firm will be the sole purchaser of the output. Furthermore, since the plant will be owned *and managed* by the tribe, the firm will be able to meet a portion of its minority set-aside requirement for sales to the federal government. Given the high unemployment rate on the reservation, the firm believes that the wage rate will be lower than it would be in the nearby metropolitan area.

The national firm also has a social agenda. Besides the explicit benefits acquired from working with a minority business, the firm's management feels a desire to help employ and develop the reservation economy. Toward this end, the firm proposes instituting a scholarship program for tribal members and is willing to make a significant investment in the tribal school system, the tribal college, and the tribal health clinic. Although these incentives may appear as inducements in the negotiation process, the national firm makes the donations without any strings attached.

The tribal government conducts a background study on the national firm and finds that everything is on the up and up. The firm is sincerely interested in investing on the reservation and is not simply looking for a quick and easy deal.

The negotiation process involves a very reasonable loan to the tribe to build the assembly plant and a straightforward contract for the output of the plant. The national firm also agrees to provide both managerial and production training for the employees. Now the tribe only has to provide an assurance that the work can be accomplished. In order to meet the production schedule, the assembly plant needs a labor supply of twenty-three welders, twelve mechanics, and forty-five other people who are able to read blueprints. The remaining staff includes two accountants, one computer programmer, two data entry personnel, and one manager. The national firm states that training is available, but the basic skills need to be available for the training. How does the tribe respond?

In most cases, the answer is that the tribe has no idea whether or not these skills are available. With a tribal population of several hundred or several thousand, it might be possible to find this many people, but . . .

In a developed community, the question of employment skills is readily answered. The community has so many metal shops and so many firms that employ mechanics and so on. But on a reservation with 40–75 percent unemployment, it is not readily known what skills are available. Thus the tribe needs to complete a labor skills assessment and inventory. A sample survey instrument is included in the appendix to this chapter.

CONCLUSION

An overall development plan for moving from the status quo to a new and positive future requires a developing economy. The development cycle model in conjunction with economic base analysis provides a paradigm for identifying those types of enterprise likely to be successful. Chapter 8 returns to the idea of designing actual community development plans.

NOTES

1. This chapter is largely based on Smith 1994a.
2. Specifically, see p. 173.
3. Nor is the reality of comparative advantage and trade a two-product process. Given the multitude of goods and services in the modern economy, the direction of trade for any one good may reverse, or trade of one specific good may simply cease as conditions change.
4. The Mentor–Protégé legislation (sec. 1207 of P.L. 99-661) allows major defense contractors to form very close linkages with small disadvantaged businesses beyond the scope of 8(A) certification. The major contractor provides tech-

nical assistance, equipment, training programs, and the like to the subcontractor. In return, the major firm is able to apply these costs—multiplied by various factors depending on the type of assistance—toward their required 5 percent set-aside. See Reed Smith et al. 1991 for more details.

5. Steve Cornell emphasized the importance of this point.

6. These data are prior to recent development activities for both tribes.

7. *E* refers to English and *H* refers to Hualapai or the local Native language.

APPENDIX

The sample labor skills survey instrument included in this appendix was developed in conjunction with work that CAIED and NEEPNAL did with the Hualapai Nation. See chapter 13 for a more detailed discussion of their relationship with the Hualapai Nation. The survey can be modified to address local needs.

Individual data (one per person 18–64)
1) Name:_____ 2) SS#:_____

3) Address:_____

_____

4) Race: _____ 5) Enrolled tribal member:_____

6) Age: _____

7) Phone:_____ 8) Sex:____ 9) Employed:_____

10) Where:_____

11) On/Off Res:_____ 12) Occupation:_____

13) Satisfied:_____ 14) Wage:_____ 15) Full/part time:_____

16) Days of work:_____ 17) Seasonal job:_____

18) Why:_____

19) Other seasonal:_____ 20) Educational level:_____

21) GED_____ 22) Bilingual: (first/second)_____

23) College major:_____ 24) Read: E/H 25) Write: E/H[7]

26) Special training:_____

_____

27) Special skills:_____

_____

Employment history:

	Dates	Employer	Duties
28) From____to____		_____	_____
29) From____to____		_____	_____
30) From____to____		_____	_____
31) From____to____		_____	_____

32) Do you have transportation?_____ _____

33) How far do you travel to work?_____ _____

34) How far would you be willing to travel to work?_____

35) Do you make any arts or craft items?_____ 36) What?_____

_____

37) If you could obtain the ideal job, what would it be?_____

38) What other jobs would you be interested in taking?_____

_____

39) What wage would be necessary?_____

40) What days of the week would you be willing to work?_____

41) What hours of the day would you be willing to work?_____

42) Would you be willing to enter a training program to enhance your reading, writing, and math skills if jobs were available after the training?_____

43) Would you be willing to enter an advanced training program to learn technical skills if jobs were available after the training?_____

44) Would you be willing to be contacted if jobs were being announced for which you have the necessary skills? If you say yes, we will create a computer file with this information. If you say no, we will delete your name and address from the file._____

45) Would you require child care to take a job?_____

46) Would you be willing to undergo training to allow you to provide child care?_____

47) If you are unemployed or are not satisfied with your current job, why do you feel you have been unable to find satisfactory employment?

    a) Have not looked

    b) No transportation

    c) No jobs available

    d) Do not have correct training/skills/education

    e) No child care

    f) Other_____

Recorder_____Recorder #_____

5

❦

Cultural Integrity
and Economic Development

Mainstream America prides itself on the melting pot philosophy and the American Dream. Any individual from anywhere can succeed with hard work and diligence.[1] The general economic success of the United States is based on these very ideals. The idea of a melting pot includes homogeneity among participants in the endeavor for success, whereas success is actually due to a mixture of people from differing backgrounds with varying ideas. Families in Texas still speak German after a hundred years, and they make wonderful sausage and breads. The Scandinavian influence in Minnesota is obvious. San Francisco is renowned for its Chinatown. Successful Koreans became vitally important during the riots in Los Angeles. And Native American arts and crafts are finding a growing worldwide market. The melting pot of America has not and should not involve making every inhabitant meet the uniform ideals of the majority powers. This is the very strength of the movement and societal structure.

Although this argument appears somewhat jaded, it is still relevant. During a public forum concerning the proposed Navajo–Hopi land settlement described in the introduction,[2] several comments were made implying the need to assimilate the Native population into the mainstream: "Why can't we all just be the same?"

Native American cultures are a positive addition to the success of the United States. They made transfers of technology and crops to early European invaders, and the Constitution is based on a Native American form of government. Without Benjamin Franklin's recognition of the power of separate states, based on the League of Nations forming the Iroquois confederacy, the United States would not have succeeded.

But the subject matter of this chapter goes beyond a simple discussion of diversity. Due the unique legal status of the reservation system, Native Americans are distinct legal and political entities as well as distinct ethnic groups. Economic activity interacting with the political systems adds to the concerns of cultural integrity. On the other hand, the distinct legal sovereignty of the First Nations provides opportunities not available to other cultural segments of the mainstream society.

This chapter addresses the importance of culture and explores how aspects of culture can be used as tools leading toward economic development and how development can be used to maintain the cultural integrity of the tribe. As previously mentioned, the culture of a society involves the language, religion, traditions, and reverence for the family and tribe by members of that society.

Several aspects of Native American cultures are vital to the current discussion and are summarized succinctly in the following extract:

> For tribal people, who see the world as a whole, the essence of our work is in its entirety. In a society where all are related, where everybody is someone else's mother, father, brother, sister, aunt or cousin, and where you cannot leave without eventually coming home, simple decisions require the approval of nearly everyone in that society. It is a society as a whole, not merely a part of it, that must survive. This is Indian understanding. It is understanding in a global sense. (First Nations Financial Project 1991, 5)

One aspect of Native American cultures originated in pre-Columbian times but also resulted from federal policies. This is the communal nature of resource allocation and decision making. Multitudes of distinct tribes in pre-Columbian times experienced intense tribal identification due to recurrent conflicts over resources. Ever fluid intertribal negotiations also made group decisions tantamount to survival and success for generally small decision-making bodies. Combine this with the extreme hardships encountered by these social groups during the military campaigns, relocation, and reservation policies of the federal government, and it becomes obvious that tribal survival was, and is, of manifest importance. Since the survival of the individual, and the individual's nuclear family, was uncertain, the tribal group became the focus of survival. Adding to the communal decision-making process is the federal policy of holding the remaining land, for most tribes, in trust for the tribe. Thus no single individual has clear and proper title to any parcel of land, meaning that decisions must be made by or for the whole tribe.[3]

It must also be pointed out that holding land in trust, or communally, is not compatible with all traditional methods of land-use allocation. Many tribes were nomadic.[4] Others had specific areas used by extended families—an ongoing point of contention in the Navajo–Hopi land settlement problem. The current situation is that the land is held in trust, and many tribes are frightened of any type of allocation scheme that holds the potential for loss of land, as during the Allotment period. For example, as I was having a conversation with Mike Her Many Horses (1992), executive director of the Oglala Sioux Tribe, his aunt overheard us discussing site leases for entrepreneurial activity. She suggested that this was not a smart idea and that we were too young to remember the Allotment period.

The tribe is at the zenith of tribal activities.[5] Perpetuating and developing the tribe is tantamount to being a member of the tribe. Marilyn Enfield (1992) explains the importance of developing her company within the context of Apache values and providing opportunities for tribal members. She mentioned that personal opportunities had been offered—well in excess of her position—but her devotion to the White Mountain Apache Tribe outweighs any and all personal advancement. Apache Aerospace is a wholly owned tribal enterprise, and Enfield got her authority directly from the chairman and the council. In other words, developing resources is not solely aimed at profitability for any one individual; rather, the enterprise is ventured for the success of the tribe.

The comments of John Bowannie (1992), president of Cochiti Community Development Corporation and former governor of the Cochiti Pueblo, about compatibility between economic activity and tribal goals bear repeating. He distinguishes between the terms culture and tradition. Traditions include activities describing the heritage of the tribe, including religious and ceremonial activities. Culture incorporates the traditions with other aspects of life such as work and regulations. Therefore, traditions are those aspects of the culture steeped in a historical basis. Bowannie further explains that while it may be difficult to merge traditional behavior with successfully competing in a market economy, it is not impossible. Furthermore, some aspects of the culture can be developed and improved when the traditions and values of the tribe are merged with an evolving economy.

The communal nature of beliefs and structure of the land base should not lead one to think that individuality and individual success are neither important nor possible on reservations. Nor should it be interpreted to mean that land and other resources are not allocated for personal use. Instead, individual behaviors are tempered by responsibilities to the tribe.[6] Marilyn Enfield explains how her upbringing was based on traditional values, which included the importance of giving back to the tribe after finishing her education. This should not be interpreted as meaning that she is unable or dissuaded from enjoying personal benefits from her work. Similarly, site leases are available for land in the Navajo Nation, and elsewhere, for profit-oriented businesses. Furthermore, the Navajo Nation is vigorously attempting to encourage individuals to apply for site leases for entrepreneurial activities.

Besides tribal affiliation and responsibilities, being a member of a unique society involves other issues. These include being fluent in the community's language and religious activities. Following explicit and implicit policies of assimilation, many tribes find themselves facing a severe reduction in the number of tribal members who are cognizant of the inner workings of their culture. Nora Garcia, former chairwoman of the Fort Mohave Tribe, said that only a few elderly members still speak the tribal language. The Navajo Nation faces a severe shortage of singers. Other tribes also face critical depletion of their cultural backgrounds.

Because of the boarding school system and other assimilation policies, young parents today either experienced the system or are the children of parents who were punished for participating in cultural activities. Therefore, a current movement reintroduces cultural activities into schools and other formal actions. In terms of language, three possible configurations exist in Indian Country. One uses English as a second language and thus must mentally translate all ideas and thoughts when speaking English: this is an individual with a traditional background. A second person must translate from English into the Native language and may feel embarrassed when addressing an audience in the Native language. The third person only knows English and does not participate in the cultural activity. But there is a sincere, and understanding, crusade to reintroduce language into many tribal and family activities. Today's parents understand what they have lost and what they must teach their children.

Another aspect of culture falls within the realm of religion. Past assimilation policies dealt serious setbacks to Native American spiritualities. However, the same type of movement that is addressing language concerns is taking up this aspect of culture as well. Unfortunately, an enormous confusion exists in this realm. A multitude of religious sects made inroads into Indian Country in the past. Because one individual may be a member of two or three churches as well as an active member in Native tradition, there is room for confusion to set in.

How can cultural activities and developing cultural integrity aid in the economic development process?[7] Without delving into the sociological aspects of self-identity and the importance of being a part of a group, I want to focus on activities involving the production of goods and services and productivity issues.

The burgeoning Native American arts and crafts industry holds immense potential for raising incomes and skill levels. Every facet of this industry holds vast potential for growth. Jerry Conover (1988) estimates that the retail arts and crafts industry in Phoenix alone generates over $180 million per year. Stimulating tourism in Indian Country, films such as *Dances with Wolves* and *Thunderheart*, popular authors such as Tony Hillerman, and the five hundredth anniversary of Columbus all increased interest in Native American cultures and the corresponding arts and crafts. The sharing of cultural artifacts extends to increasing markets, for example, of Hopi blue corn.

The discussion above concerning adaptation and the need for compatibility among subsystems of culture extends to many aspects of Native

American arts and crafts. Although many Native American artifacts have symbolic and spiritual aspects, much creativity and adaptation takes place in the production of these goods. Native American themes and styles are prevalent in items made for aesthetic and not spiritual purposes. This is what recasting the idea of progress to include Native American ideals means above. As long as Native people make the decisions concerning what is seemly, development activities can be culturally appropriate.

There has been much controversy and discussion concerning the arts and crafts industry. As discussed in the introduction, federal law dictates what can and cannot be sold as "authentic" Indian art. The concern over imported products using Native American designs is also worthy of extended discussion, but these issues fall beyond the scope of our current purpose: self-determined production of what each individual deems appropriate.

In addition to arts, crafts, and other cultural products, tourism is a growing factor on many reservations. The Navajo Nation is vigorously studying the potential market.[8] Tourism includes activities ranging from sightseeing visits to viewing and participating in cultural activities such as dances, rodeos, and powwows. Native American ideals can be included in tourism plans that reduce the negative aspects stemming from the industry by focusing on community-based tourism planning. By allowing local communities to design and plan local tourism activities—with guidance, integration strategies, and support from the tribe—the results of the development process can be compatible with the remainder of the societal goals.

Another avenue for economic development based on cultural integrity is education. Having more cultural and language courses taught in the schools and community colleges on reservations increases demand for tribal members as teachers. These teachers may either replace non-Indian teachers or augment the current faculty. In either case, the income earned by tribal members rises. A secondary impact includes the well-known conclusion that having teachers of the same ethnicity as the students significantly improves the success of the students. Also, as students begin to see their culture as an asset, their self-esteem and interest in success increases.

A combination of education and tourism is evidenced at Diné College (DC, formerly Navajo Community College), as well as other tribal schools. DC teaches Elderhostel and other groups about Navajo traditions and craftwork. For example, DC provides regular workshops at the Tsaile campus for faculty and staff of Northern Arizona University (NAU). These three-day workshops cover topics from Navajo spirituality to lifestyles in a hogan with an extended family to language difficulties to cultural norms concerning respect of elders (i.e., faculty). This last point is vital when teaching Navajos because this respect precludes asking the faculty member for help; therefore, the professor should approach the student and engage in a conversation leading to an offer of help. Since NAU enrolls a large number of Navajo students, these workshops are intended to help the NAU faculty and staff understand their students' culture of origin. Other courses and workshops are, or could be, offered to different audiences.

Besides specific markets based on selling cultural artifacts, entertainment, or knowledge, Native American cultural norms also have a potential for increased productivity in the workplace. What is the Native American work ethic? A nearly universal cultural aspect of Native America is an understanding of the world as a holistic entity. From this viewpoint, workers are able to see their work as important and vital to the success of the enterprise, for example, understanding how a quality thermal blanket for an Apache helicopter enhances the profitability of the enterprise, which in turn leads to an increase in the tribe's revenues, which in turn leads to the betterment of the tribal members because, perhaps, a new service can be provided that increases their incentive to produce a quality thermal blanket. Large corporations doing business with tribal enterprises are generally very satisfied with the quality of the production done by these enterprises *when there is sufficient management and managerial discretion.*[9]

Native American culture also has possible influences in the managerial area. Even as production workers are able to see the holistic importance of their output, management is also able to view the holistic importance of employees. Marilyn Enfield mentions several aspects of this when describing her plans for Apache Aerospace. Besides explaining the planned diversification, she reveals plans to provide day care for her employees. She also mentions the idea of tracking employees' children's progress in school and providing incentives for success. Furthermore, she vigorously engages in many cultural activities, which are also available to her employees. This last point highlights the problems inherent with non-Indian management. Since most Native American spiritual and cultural events do not follow the mainstream work week, tensions can arise when an employee has to decide between the job (or school) and family responsibilities. Having Indian management, which understands the holistic nature of being a being, alleviates these problems by letting the employee return home for activities besides weddings and funerals, and thus increases productivity through a better working atmosphere. Robert White provides an example of this:[10]

Indian funerals here take three days, five days sometimes, and if you're a sixty-fourth cousin, you show up, whether the factory has a deadline or not. I'm not saying give up our traditions. We're actually exploring trade-off time for workers, so they can spend more time at important gatherings. I know they're willing to do that, even though Russ says in other plants he's worked in it would never happen.

This past Christmas, it all started coming together. We had a big pre-Christmas deadline, and we'd been threatening for a week to make everybody work on Saturday and during their holiday week if we didn't make it. Well, everybody got all of their work done, and Dorothy and I were sitting back like big bosses, watching them work and take all their own responsibility. It was just great. We all left early.

Before this discussion is closed, one vital point needs to be made. I am not suggesting that all cultural and spiritual aspects of a tribe be sold or marketed. The Havasupai, Hualapai, and Hopi are among those tribes choosing not to market their entire culture or resources. This choice is one steeped in self-determination practices. For example, Hopi kachina dolls traditionally are not made for their marketability. Indeed, many members of the tribe strenuously protest the sale of these commodities because of the strong spiritual importance of the kachinas. If the individual, or tribe, decides that marketing artifacts is not culturally appropriate, then so be it. An alternative would be to use the required skills to carve other marketable products. This would avoid a conflict but would still provide increased development.

Native American cultures are a vital portion of the overall makeup of the United States. That these cultures still exist as identifiable, distinct societies in the wake of past assimilation and genocidal policies of the federal government proves their viability and strength. This same viability and strength hold the potential for economic growth and success. Past policies have produced third world–style standards of living. The availability of welfare programs and alcohol has exacerbated the effect of past failures to produce the current appalling situation on many reservations. However, the cultural aspects described above can lead the First Nations out of their dire straits, *if they are able to self-determine their own futures* by adopting a Native American ideal of progress when designing their strategies.

Of course, the issues of self-determination are complex and very fuzzy. Like the pendulum of federal policy, which swings between self-determination and control, the issues of true self-determination and sovereignty complicate the current discussion. We are currently focusing on an idealized scenario in which First Nations people are truly able to make the kinds of decisions described in this discussion.

A well-developed plan of action incorporating import replacement, product innovation, and export development is needed to jump-start the economy. No one business venture is the key; rather, a variety of enterprises making use of the available resources and making use of the agglomerating factors between the enterprises is required to get the economy moving in a positive direction.

Understanding development as a process rather than a black or white phenomenon leaves the planner with an optimistic vantage point on the possibilities of success. It is this process orientation that holds the focal point of this volume. The development cycle model provides a paradigm for the expansion process, which puts us in a position to fully understand growth possibilities.

White (1990) concludes his work by recognizing that the four reservations in his study have only begun to reach a point at which they can address the serious socioeconomic problems resulting from years of inept federal policies. After twenty years, or more, of success relative to other reservations, the four subject reservations are only beginning to address the difficult issues of suicide, alcoholism, diabetes, low life expectancy, and the like. Without a lengthy time horizon, there is truly little hope for other less successful reservations.

Tribal sovereignty and self-determination are the mainstays of current development plans. These goals can only be truly realized if and when the population becomes self-supporting and the tribe overcomes its dependency on the federal government. By developing a vigorous cycle of economic growth, the tribe will be able to fulfill these goals.

To fully develop the available human and natural resources, the tribe must do the following. First, it must formulate a positive atmosphere for growth. This includes supporting and maintaining a stable tribal government. It may be necessary for tribal members to forgo short-term political nitpicking in order to develop long-term stability. Second, the tribe needs to actively recruit outside investors and partners in the development process. Again, this may allow for short-term interference in tribal activities, but the long-term gain will offset this disruption. Third, the tribe must aid tribal members in their individual entrepreneurial activities. This may include streamlining the inevitable red tape as well as providing technical assistance. The tribe also needs to invest in its members by reducing the restrictions on site leases and the like. Fourth, the tribe must develop a comprehensive plan of action, but this plan must be flexible enough to address alternatives as they become apparent.

A mixture of tribal enterprises, partnerships, and private enterprise is required for development. The tribe must negotiate from a position of strength as a sovereign nation and must encourage partnerships between tribal members and outside investors. This combination of activity can lead to a vigorous cycle of economic growth. The resulting education, training, risk taking, income growth, and cultural integrity will be well worth the investment as the tribe becomes a truly sovereign nation determining its own path.

As a final note, the tribe *must* take the position of searching for long-term growth. To move from a current state with high unemployment, and all the concomitant social problems, to the growth and prosperity of true self-determination and self-sufficiency, a time horizon of at least fifteen to twenty years is necessary. Native Americans are renowned for our concern about past and future generations. The sacrifice and efforts of the current generation will, if properly formulated, allow future generations to regain their hold on sovereignty and culture. All First Nations have the ability and determination to see this dream come true.

When Native ideals and cultural norms direct the development process, progress can be achieved. The cultural capital of the First Nations can be utilized to guide the implementation process. Questions of true sovereignty and government-to-government relations certainly restrict some kinds of activity. However, the ideal of self-determination certainly allows tribes to say no even though they may not always be allowed to say yes.

NOTES

1. This chapter is largely based on Smith 1994b.

2. November 3, 1992. This was held in the Walkup Skydome on the campus of Northern Arizona University after it became apparent the Flagstaff City Hall would not be large enough. See Davison 1992 for the consensus statement generated during the forum.

3. These restrictions and decisions are more restrictive and communal than zoning ordinances passed by city governments.

4. See Medicine Crow 1992. He details the Crow migration story beginning around A.D. 1550.

5. Again, the term tribe is also used to mean clan, band, or village. The level of allegiance toward the federally recognized tribal identity varies greatly.

6. Again, generalities are not intended as global behavior patterns. The well-known case of Peter McDonald and his chairmanship of the Navajo Nation is a glaring counterexample of the behavior being described.

7. The next chapter turns this question around.

8. Tony Skrelunas, Grand Canyon Trust, interviews, May–June 1992. The discussion of community-based tourism stems from an ongoing project of the Grand Canyon Trust.

9. This observation is based on field experience with several enterprises. Examples are Apache Aerospace, Tooh Dineh Industries, and Hopi Technologies. Problems can occur in connection with inexperienced management or interference from the tribal government. See Cameron 1988, 1990; and Diamant 1988.

10. Bernyce Courtney, co–plant manager of the Warm Springs Apparel Industries, as quoted in White 1990, 224. Russ Winslow is the plant manager. He is non-Indian. Dorothy Pedersen is also non-Indian.

6

❦

Economic Development and Cultural Integrity

Economic development is merely a means to an end.[1] In and of itself, development should not be the goal of any tribe or society. Rather, the development of resources leads to a higher standard of living, increased cultural vitality, and greater freedom to make choices concerning the future. In this chapter I focus on how these linkages strengthen the cultures of the First Nations.

When discussing economic development, President John Yellow Bird Steele (1992) of the Oglala Sioux Tribe on the Pine Ridge Reservation explained the importance of developing jobs and income because of their *social* importance. He said it was not hard to understand that when you wake up in the morning realizing that "not only is today going to be like this, but tomorrow is going to be like yesterday too. So you go out and get a bottle." He further stated that tribal members are "interested in federal service jobs, and not the goals, services and roles of those jobs." Since federal service jobs are essentially the only jobs available and the bureaucracy stifles the possibility of personal progress, the only purpose of holding a job is to get a paycheck. To correct these problems, he stated, "we need our own money here. And jobs." Compare these societal goals and difficulties with the discussion of Apache Aerospace. Clearly, the lack of economic development at Pine Ridge has an adverse influence on cultural activity if the purpose of existence is simply to get through the day to face tomorrow. Apache Aerospace, however, is profitable and expanding. When economic activities are not available, the incompatibility between the subsystems of the society throws everything out of sync, thereby resulting in a diminishing of those subsystems. Conversely, when eco-

71

nomic activity is available and is designed in conjunction with other tribal goals, all aspects of the society progress.

In order to engage in cultural activities, it is first necessary to provide for basic needs: food, shelter, and clothing. Once the basic needs are taken care of, a certain amount of disposable resources must be available for cultural activities. Resources may be measured in dollars, hours, sheep, physical energy, or interest. Furthermore, the individual engaging in cultural activities must have enough self-interest and self-esteem to participate in those activities. Given the extreme poverty and concomitant social problems on most reservations, it is not surprising that many First Nations face diminishing local interest in their cultures. How can economic development lead to the advancement and integrity of indigenous cultures? The answer is simple: provide the necessary disposable resources while designing economic activity compatible with the underlying code of values. (While the answer is simple, the practice is not!)

Native American economies have four distinct sets of resources available for potential development: cultural, natural, human, and capital (funding). Again, it is important to recognize that a decision *not* to develop some resources is a self-determined choice. The decisions should be based on the compatibility issues previously mentioned. The cultural resources were discussed above and natural resources will be discussed in the following section. The current focus is on human and capital resources.

Unemployment on reservations typically exceeds 30 percent and often exceeds 50 percent. This, of course, does not include discouraged workers or those not intrigued enough to venture into the workforce.[2] Nor does this total include those tribal members who have left the reservation for greener pastures. Clearly, a human capital surplus exists on the reservations. As more and more young people earn high school diplomas and more of them attend college and university, the skill level of the population increases. This untapped resource holds the potential for drastic increases in local output of goods and services.[3]

Marilyn Enfield (1992) understands that these are the types of jobs needed on reservations. "Just as in Third World countries, we need to start with 'cut and sew' work. Then as our skill levels increase, we can move to more advanced manufacturing techniques." The planned diversification of Apache Aerospace is aimed at this very type of enrichment. As progress is made in terms of output and skill level, a concomitant increase in wage rates and hours worked—still being competitive—will occur, thereby increasing the level of disposable resources available for cultural and other activities.

Minimum-wage jobs are not the long-term solution to problems of poverty and low income. Viewed from a short-term perspective, the only jobs that could be successfully created would be low-skill occupations with little room for advancement or raises. A long-run approach, however, views these entry-level jobs as being useful in starting the development process.

The development process is just that: a process. Moving from the status quo of depression and poverty, a growing economy can sustain the population, thus allowing the social and cultural aspects of the society to flourish. For example, retail services provide entry-level jobs. These will lead to bookkeeping and inventory skills development, as well as other job skills required for running retail outlets. Employment in the retail sector is also likely to encourage entrepreneurship in the future, which is facilitated by on-the-job training and experience.

Given these entry-level jobs and the agglomerating factors between enterprises, coincidental development of a group of activities could provide the initial force that leads to a self-sustaining cycle of vigorous growth. In other words, the entry-level jobs need to be identified as an initial stepping-stone leading to continued progress. Understanding the progression of time toward the seventh generation provides a Native American ideal compatible with progress.

Extended discussions of capital formation and funding in Indian Country are available elsewhere.[4] Several sources of capital and capital funding are available to tribes and tribal members. One of the most important sources of potential funding was mentioned above: trust accounts. True self-determination implies tribes being able to manage their own resources, including trust accounts. Since these accounts total in excess of $2 billion, these funds could be used to leverage several more billions of dollars for economic development programs and enterprises. Recent reports concerning the extraordinary ineptitude of the federal government's trust activity surely point toward the need to allow self-determined management of these funds. Additionally, sources such as the First Nations Financial Project are increasing making funds available for micro, small, and large enterprises.

Other sources of capital are partnership agreements with major manufacturers. For example, McDonnell-Douglas owns much of the machinery used by Apache Aerospace. Programs such as the Mentor-Protégé legislation (P.L. 101-510, sec. 831) are designed to make this type of arrangement beneficial to both parties.[5] Similarly, outside businesses can be invited onto the reservations. An example of this is the Bashas grocery stores in Navajo communities. The outside corporation negotiated with the Navajo Nation to lease the land and then invested its own capital funds in the project.

There is also potential to increase the utilization of existing capital. For example, the Hualapai Nation has several industrial sewing machines and two lapidary machines simply collecting dust. This capital stock could be used in some sort of enterprise, perhaps producing decorative blouses, employing several tribal members. As with the stock of human capital available for economic development, there is no lack of available capital or capital funding that *could* be made available to the tribes for developing their economies.[6]

Once economies begin to develop and disposable incomes increase, a concomitant increase in cultural activities may occur. Classic supply-and-demand analysis identifies several examples of this. One reason for the declining number of singers within the Navajo population is the low pay. The training and commitment necessary for this occupation is very extensive and lengthy. The ceremonies presented by the singers last several days and involve feeding a large extended family during the ceremony. Thus, the family hosting the ceremony needs a large cache of disposable resources. Benedek provides the following:

> Ella tells Bessie that she plans to call her sisters in California and ask them to save about a couple of hundred dollars so they can all pitch in for some of the ceremonies they need. Ella says, "You know those arrows over our front door, on the inside? Well, they were put there four years ago. Every four years, you're supposed to have a renewal for them. I told my mom she should have it done soon. It costs from eight hundred to a thousand dollars. Those things, the jewelry that is passed down, we shouldn't pawn for money or for food. We've been doing that. I told her we shouldn't be doing that. We also used to have a Beauty Way for my mom every four years on Mother's Day. Between those years we'd have a peyote ceremony for her. We haven't done that. We should have a Beauty Way for her to put her in harmony with nature and everything around her. (1992, 102–3)

Given the levels of poverty and the lack of economic activity, current circumstances lower the number of families able to hold these ceremonies and thus reduce the income levels of the singers. As a result, singers usually have to hold other jobs for the income. Clearly, this leads to a reduction in the number of people involved in the necessary training. It should be noted, however, this does not imply a lack of interest in cultural activities or ceremonies; rather, the population lacks resources to pursue interests beyond their basic human needs. But as incomes rise as a result of increased economic activity, more families will be able to afford ceremonies and thus demand will go up for singers, followed by a corresponding increase in the number of individuals willing and able to become singers.

A similar story is true in the markets for arts and crafts. Because of the historical marketing structure of traders, trading posts, and roadside stands, artisans spend a great deal of their time marketing their output. A typical story is of a weaver driving five hundred miles round-trip to sell a single rug for, say, $300. Clearly, the transaction is not profitable. Given the time required to produce the natural dies and wool used in weaving, and the time required to weave the rug, the weaver typically earns less than $1 per hour, perhaps losing money after the marketing costs are subtracted from the selling price. Developing a modern marketing structure, such as Navajo Arts and Crafts Enterprise, increases wage rates for weavers, thereby increasing the number of tribal members training for this occupation. Currently, many weavers, much like the singers, pursue their craft part time or as a hobby. Thus an improved marketing structure, an example of economic development, will lead to an increase in the cultural activities of arts and crafts production.[7] Incidentally, creating a marketing system designed around Native American ideals would allow for increased freedom in product design. At the moment, design is usually stipulated by current and past non-Indian trader dictates.

A third example of how increasing disposable income increases the cultural integrity of the First Nations is the powwow. Besides drawing tourists, these events are socially important activities as extended families travel to attend them. The costs involve include the design and production of extravagant costumes, travel, food, lodging, and the like. Drum groups must be paid, and facilities must be made available. Thus an increase in disposable income will lead to greater demand for powwow activities, which will stimulate interest in the cultural activities of dancing and drumming, including costume design.

Therefore, economic development can lead to increased participation in cultural activities. Besides the examples of spirituality, symbology, and social events, the characteristics detailed above language and history—also see increased interest and activity. Furthermore, as incomes rise tribal governments will pay less attention to the day-to-day issues of jobs, housing, and poverty, allowing them to address important issues such as constitutional reform. The cookie cutter IRA (Indian Reorganization Act) constitutions can then be amended, reflecting cultural aspects of tribal governance instead of BIA (Bureau of Indian Affairs) aspects. The goal of economic development is increasing cultural integrity and identity within the local tribe, and it is not aimed at simply merging tribal resources with the mainstream economy. Pre-Columbian societies were viable and growing with trade and resource development. The inherent principles of economic production were present in the cultural activities. Two hundred years of federal policy restricted both the economic activity and the cultural integrity of the First Nations; however, our indigenous cultures are renewing their identities and becoming trading partners within the global economy. The goal of current economic development strategies is revitalized economies stimulating cultural identity.

NOTES

1. This chapter is largely based on Smith 1994b.

2. It should also be noted that a large "underground" economy primarily involving the production, sale, and barter of arts, crafts, hunting, and agricultural products exists. In some communities, particularly Alaskan ones, this sector may constitute a substantial segment of the economic system.

3. Of course, our discussion ignores the vast "brain drain" that occurs, which results in further diminished resources. This issue is addressed in detail in chapter 12.

4. In addition to the references listed above, see Festa and St. George 1988, Ludwig and Schowalter 1988, and Monrad (1988).

5. See Reed et al. (1991) for details.

6. The above discussion is not meant to imply that economic development is an easy task. (See the papers mentioned above for descriptions of the severe difficulties faced by tribal governments.) Rather, the scope of this chapter focuses on the issue of the linkages between economic and cultural development; the obvious questions are left to other works. Issues of sovereignty, immunity, and other aspects of attracting capital funding are briefly discussed in chapter 11.

7. It should be noted that a large body of cultural symbology exists in the production of these products.

7

The Environment and Natural Resources: Some Native Ideas

Perhaps the one area of potential progress that most closely shows the possible compatibility between economic development and the other subsystems of Native American cultures lies in the environmental arena. Instead of tribes simply being assimilated into an industrial capitalistic system, Native American ideals can be used to design a new type of system that incorporates competitive behavior, social compatibility and adaptation, and environmental concerns. This chapter discusses some of the environmental issues.

In 1992 Vice President Al Gore closed an article with the following paragraph:

> What is needed, finally, is this: an ecological perspective that does not treat Earth as something separate from human civilization. We, too, are part of the whole, and looking at the whole ultimately means looking at ourselves. If we do not see that we are a powerful natural force like the winds and the tides, we cannot see how we threaten to push Earth out of balance. (1992, 27)

Native Americans have a cultural basis for understanding the holistic nature of the Earth and human activity. Perhaps this is best described by Larry Echohawk (1992) addressing Iroquoian beliefs: "In our way of life, in our government, with every decision we make, we always keep in mind the seventh generation to come. When we walk upon the Earth, we always plant our feet carefully because we know the faces of our future generations are looking up at us from beneath the ground."

The international conference in Rio de Janeiro and similar events mirror long-held Native American understandings that humanity exists in conjunction with the rest of the planet (universe). The indigenous belief that the People are caretakers of Mother Earth becomes vitally relevant and important, since the Western belief that the earth is to be despoiled and used for human consumption has resulted in severe environmental problems, some with global proportions.

As mentioned in chapter 2, Native Americans have long managed and cultivated natural resources. This chapter extends the earlier discussion by expanding the concepts developed by Talcott Parsons and Richard Norgaard to elucidate the importance of merging indigenous ideals with developing tribal resources. The importance of human interaction with the environment, and vice versa, is the focus of this chapter.

Indeed, much of the dialogue about saving the ancient forests of the Northwest and other places seems to neglect the fact that these forests have been managed and utilized for thousands of years. Only during the reservation period have these forests been essentially free to grow without human intervention. Maintaining these supposed wilderness areas free from human interaction is the Western philosophy that separates humans from the rest of nature. Some of what were envisioned as "natural" ecosystems actually deteriorated when human management was limited.[1] Thus questions of natural resource management should not concern utilization versus nonuse; rather, answers need to include caretaking and stewardship.

Indian land is rich in natural resources, including flora and fauna, water, minerals, geothermal energy, and scenic vistas. Self-determination policies imply resident tribes being able to make decisions concerning the cultivation of these resources. Past management of these resources by the federal government has resulted in serious environmental problems. On the other hand, tribally managed resources are among the most profitable and environmentally sound enterprises in existence. For example, the best elk hunting in the world is available on the land of the White Mountain Apache Tribe (Kalt 1987). Tribal management of the elk herd incorporates an understanding of the holistic nature of herd, forest, and long-term conservation. Matthew Krepps (1991) shows that tribally managed forestry programs are more profitable than BIA-managed programs.

Undeveloped and underdeveloped resources available on Indian lands are not the result of poor tribal management; rather, they are the result of nontribal management. Either resources have been managed by federal bureaucrats or development has not been available. Given the environmental outcomes of past federal policies, perhaps it is beneficial that many resources have been left untapped. Even when tribal stewardship has seemingly resulted in environmental damage, this can still be traced to federal policy. Like overgrazing on federal lands, overgrazing on Indian lands results from a classic tragedy of the commons stemming from the trust nature of land holdings and nonmarket allocation of resources.

Development of natural resources can lead either to conflict (similar to those mentioned above concerning federal Indian policy) or to compatibility with the overall code of values of the indigenous culture. A holistic understanding of nature and a reverence for the land can lead tribes to make environmentally and culturally sound decisions. When an incompatibility between development and the other subsystems exists, then the *tribe* must reach a point of compatibility by either altering or refusing the development strategy.

Two types of resources are available for development: renewable and extractive. Traditional culture recognizes that renewable resources are to be managed with the understanding that short-term consumption should not occur at the cost of long-term sustained use. Resources are to be harvested but cared for in order to maintain the continued health of the ecosystem. Resources ranging from salmon to forests to herd animals are considered renewable resources to be used today, tomorrow, and by the seventh generation.

Examples that show how development strategies can take environmental concerns into account involve the Puyallup Tribe and the Warm Springs Reservation. Paul Nissenbaum and Paul Shadle (1992) explain that the land-use policy of the Puyallup Tribe takes into account any and all impacts that potential land-use plans will have on the fisheries. Since this tribe has a significant cultural attachment to salmon fishing, it is vitally important that all impacts on the fisheries be either minimized or avoided completely. Robert White (1990, 230–32) discusses the cultural importance that the Warm Springs Reservation places on Mount Jefferson and that led it to deny the development of a ski enterprise. Furthermore, the reservation protects some of the forest because of past historical importance. Finally, the tribe takes into account the interactions of the ecosystem when determining what portions of the forest to harvest.

Extractive resources present other issues. Many tribes consider mining activities damaging to Mother Earth. As already noted, the Havasupai turned down an extensive uranium mining operation, believing that it would damage the cultural integrity of their beliefs concerning the Earth. Other tribes consider mining an acceptable activity, *if the surface features are restored and damage is kept to a minimum through modern reclamation procedures.* Deciding to extract minerals, therefore, is a decision the individual tribe must make based on compatibility with cultural, economic, and spiritual beliefs. Of course, this only happens when the tribe is self-determined. A counterexample is the use of Hopi water by Peabody Coal to slurry coal to Nevada.

This holistic vision is environmentally sound, economically profitable, and culturally based. Since the global economy is beginning to accept these long-held Native American principles, the strength and power of ancient visions are demonstrated. Once again, the essence of economic principles found within the indigenous cultures is becoming prevalent in the development of the global economy.

SOCIAL THEORY AND THE ENVIRONMENT

Given the evidence above, pre-contact Native American societies clearly developed and maintained extensive economic systems. Furthermore, they did so within an environmental philosophy that allowed the European settlers/invaders to believe that the environment upon contact was of pristine and primeval quality uninfluenced by humans. The evidence is also clear that the Native American societies, with their extensive economies, had had substantial influence on the environment. In chapter 2 I described how and why Native American social systems have faltered in the face of two hundred years of federal policy. In chapter 5 I explained how indigenous cultures can lead the Native American reservations toward successful futures by developing their economies. More importantly, in chapter 6 I also argued that developing reservation economies is vital to sustaining and developing Native American cultural identities.

For reasons akin to the problems facing Native American reservations, the mainstream economy in the United States and the global economy in both industrialized and developing countries have reached a point of disequilibrium. Among the reasons for this imbalance is the treatment of the environment.[2] Following the previous chapters, the current chapter invokes Parsonian theory of social development to explain how the ideas of economic development can be advanced with Native American environmental ideas.

The structural compatibility among subsystems is often severely disrupted, and the resulting discord can cause drastic alterations in the interaction among subsystems. As indicated above, prior to contact, "inheritors of long traditions from their forebears, they tried to live in harmony and balance with the earth and the sky and take care of them both, each in their own way, for the well-being of their peoples and those who follow them" (Iverson 1992, 117). However, the harmony and balance was upset with contact. Calvin Martin (1978) presents a controversial hypothesis that the subarctic fur trade was successful because of the migration of European diseases prior to formal contact. According to Martin, the numerous deaths caused by migrating epidemics were blamed on animal spirits. As retribution for this attack on humans, the Native Americans took revenge on the wildlife. Since this was closely followed by the European traders' arrival, Martin argues, the fur trade was jump-started because the symbiosis between man and nature seemed to have been disrupted.

Martin's hypothesis has been attacked on several levels. (See Krech III 1981 and Thistle 1986, for example.) However, the aftermath of the beginning of the fur trade certainly introduced serious discord among the social subsystems. Martin (1978, 10) indicates that as prices rose early in the fur trade period, fewer pelts were delivered for trade. In essence, this backward bending supply curve (Martin incorrectly describes it as simply inelastic) is a common phenomenon in labor markets when income is well above subsistence levels. However, as the fur trade proceeded, the alterations in society moved the subsystems toward a new equilibrium.

Martin (1981), responding to critiques of his hypothesis, indicates that overexploitation of fur bearers occurred because of the increased availability of imports. Consistent with the rationale for conservation given above, the availability of alternative food sources meant conservation to avoid the "wages of poverty" was no longer a pressing need. Arthur Ray continues with a description of how the change in social environment altered the structural compatibility. "As noted, when country food stocks (wild) declined, native people had to spend more time searching for food; therefore, they had less time to devote to trapping activity. . . . HBC [Hudson's Bay Company] imported flour and sold it well below cost to Indians. It was hoped that this subsidy would encourage trapping" (1984, 9). Ray goes on to explain that a system of credit led to a dependence by the native people, which led to a "trading post subsistence" as the fur trade declined. Of course, the symbiosis between the trading post subsistence combined with a declining availability of game, Martin argues, led to a welfare mentality within the subarctic populations.

I have argued (Smith 1994b) a similar case concerning reservation populations in the United States. Mark Plotkin (1993) argues likewise concerning tribes in the Amazon rain forest. As discussed above, the movement of various subsystems is not necessarily toward any type of optimal solution. Rather, the dislocations among aspects of the social fabric can lead to a spiraling down as adjustments occur.

Boyce Richardson explains that the interaction among various subsystems is essential to "renewal" on a Mikmaq Reservation: "They talk of 'unlocking the minds' of the Mikmaq people from their psychology of dependency, of taking the people back to 'the social, economic, political and spiritual order we had before the coming of the white man'" (1993, 75).

According to my social theory, the very form of an individual's utility function is determined, in part, by the interaction among the various social subsystems. Furthermore, the interaction between the economic subsystem and the remaining subsystems in part determines the very methods of production and distribution of output. Of particular importance is the interaction between the economic and environmental subsystems.

The difference between the traditional Native American environmental views and traditional mainstream environmental views is of particular importance. Ronald Trosper (1992) discusses the importance of various mind-sets and the successfulness of economic development programs. In terms of environmental mind-sets, he distinguishes between worldviews in which humans either live in harmony with nature—a Native American perspective—or exercise mastery over nature—a mainstream perspective. Dee Brown (1970, 8) explains how the doctrine of Manifest Destiny led the European settlers to view America as a place for conquest. Not only were the Indians to be removed, assimilated, or conquered, but the land itself was to be reaped of all its riches. Besides the treatment of the Native Americans, this doctrine also led to the 1872 federal mining law and the Homestead Act: the mainstream worldview was (and is) one that includes using anything the land can provide. Countering this worldview is a Native American one. Perhaps the best terminology is the Navajo concept of Harmony. Saying that someone "walks in Harmony" is one of the greatest compliments that can be bestowed upon a person. The phrase means the person is in harmony with the spirit, natural, and temporal worlds.

Currently, mainstream societies are growing more and more concerned with environmental issues. From water to air to noise pollution, from the devastation of land, wildlife, and flora to toxic waste buildup, from soil erosion to rampant starvation, from the diminishing ozone shield to the prospect of global warming, the global community is becoming increasingly concerned with the effects of pure economic growth and development. The problems concerning the environment are pervading both federal and global discussions. Local concerns are commonplace in small town newspapers. Clearly, the economic and environmental subsystems of the mainstream society have reached a point of disequilibrium.

The structural incompatibility of mainstream society occurred as a direct result of the very process that produced success. Dennis Pirages indicates that "discovery of the fossil fuel benefits and new technologies caused a 'great transformation' in the norms, values, morals and growth expectations within newly industrialized societies" (1977a, 1).

In other words, as production and consumption increased so drastically during the twentieth century, other subsystems evolved to new levels as the rapidly expanding economic subsystem changed. However, these changes have had deleterious influences on the environment. Now, as the century turns, environmental concerns are gaining more and more importance. In the past, when resources were exhausted—buffalo, timber, and oil fields—new resources were substituted according to marginal rates of substitution or new technologies were developed. The current status of environmental concern goes beyond exhaustion issues: modern economic production results in severe, complex, and perhaps irreparable damage to extensive ecosystems. Increasingly, recognizing this causes increased debate, policy analysis, and policy design. In other words: *mainstream society is wrestling with the problem of regaining a structural compatibility.*

ENVIRONMENTAL ECONOMICS: CURRENT THOUGHT

Although the discussion between growth and the environment may be said to have begun with Thomas Malthus, it is usually dated to Arthur Pigou. As

William Baumol and Wallace Oates (1988) indicate, economists were seemingly well prepared for the "environmental revolution." A survey of the vast literature concerning methods of analyzing and measuring environmental impacts and corrections is well beyond the scope of this chapter, but a very brief survey of the main streams of thought is relevant. Maureen Cropper and Wallace Oates (1992) provide a detailed survey of the literature, and their eighteen-column bibliography furnishes an extensive reading list.

Beginning with Pigou, moving through the Coase theorem concerning market efficiency, and being thoroughly discussed by Baumol and Oates, the theory of externalities has dominated economic thought concerning environmental issues. The idea of internalizing external effects of economic activity supposedly leads to a social optimum when marginal social cost is equated with marginal social benefit. Although modern analysis is more complex than this simple description, the intent remains the same: to identify the extent of the costs of economic activity and match them up with the perceived benefits. This cost-benefit approach has been used extensively for a wide variety of production and development issues. In theory, once property rights have been assigned and costs and benefits identified, a social welfare maximizing agenda is reached. However useful this body of thought has been, many economists—as well as researchers in the sister disciplines—have pointed out flaws in the approach.

Reminiscent of Norgaard's comments concerning the idea of progress as the default assumption of Western societies, the always controversial Paul Ehrlich (1989) argues that the neoclassical analysis of development and externalities is founded on two commonly unrecognized axioms: resources are infinite and substitution can occur when any one resource is exhausted. Kenneth Boulding implicitly foreshadowed Ehrlich when he stated that "this idea that both production and consumption are bad things rather than good things is very strange to economists" (1966, 10). These ideas have led to the sustainable economy school. Some believe that activity can continue to grow, while others argue for a leveling off of activity. Instead of focusing on price mechanisms, this body of thought focuses on production limits, birth rate limits, depletion quotas, and the like.[3]

Countering Norgaard's ideas concerning progress and specifically attacking Erhlich's body of work, Ronald Bailey (1993) writes against any recognition of environmental problems. The title of his book clearly indicates his preferences: *ECOSCAM*. Bailey employs the externalities and property rights concepts. On a single page he requires all three of the assumptions under discussion. Two pages later he falls back on the Judeo-Christian concept of Manifest Destiny.

In discussing the potentials for increasing food production, Bailey argues that "crop yields will drop by a minuscule 2 percent over the next century. Of course, one prediction *you can bank* on is that vast technical improvements in farming will be made over the next hundred years" (1993, 48, emphasis added). Bailey merely asserts the implied assumption that growth and progress are inevitable. He finds no need for evidence or discussion: quite simply, it will occur.

In the very next paragraph, Bailey discusses soil salinization. "Soil sal-
ization caused by irrigation can be *reduced* by new sprinkler, drip, and
trailing-tube irrigation" (1993, 48, emphasis added). The rate at which
salinization occurs can be reduced, but the soil will eventually become
unusable. The new technologies he suggests are implicitly invoking the
substitutability assumption. He concludes the paragraph: "Farmers can
also plant salt-tolerant crop varieties *in the future*" (1993, 48, emphasis
added). He further *assumes* that substitutability and scientific progress
will provide a solution for soil that has been contaminated through unnat-
ural ecosystem management.

In the next paragraph Bailey continues that "farmers respond to prices
like anyone else: once it costs too much to pump water from a shrinking
aquifer, the land is no longer irrigated. Scientists are also in the process of
devising ways to recharge aquifers" (1993, 48).

So, according to Bailey, market forces work. But he does not address the
result that once it becomes too expensive to irrigate, the land is no longer
productive. Presumably he assumes the land can then be put to some
other crop or use. Of course, he again places heavy emphasis on scientific
progress solving the problem.

Two pages later Bailey asserts that "he [Ehrlich] equates humans and
animals, arguing that what is true of animals must also be true of human
beings. Consequently, he treats human beings as if we were just a clever
herd of gazelles limited by the earth's 'carrying capacity'" (1993, 50).

Obviously Bailey firmly believes that human cleverness is able to expand
the limits of the Earth's carrying capacity. Recalling the discussion of Trosper's remarks concerning mind-sets (1992), Bailey clearly founds his comments on a belief that humans have a mastery over nature, whereas Ehrlich
accepts a worldview that has humans living in conjunction with nature.

The disagreement among schools of thought has been argued to rest on
an undervaluation of resources, including a misconception of production
as measured by GDP, differing discount rates, uncertainty concerning
inventories of resources, and the like. The property rights school, focusing
on internalized externalities, views development as possible and valuable
as long as its true costs and benefits can be identified. The sustainability
school focuses on limits to growth inherent in a closed system. Although
both of these schools of thought, as well as many other less familiar ones,
have valuable conclusions and analytical techniques, recent research has
pointed to the fact that something is missing in the overall scheme.

Ronald Coase (1988, 15) argued for institutional and structural change
when the real-world aspects of transactions costs are included in the
analysis. "It is quite understandable, if I am right, current economic analysis is incapable of handling many of the problems to which it purports to
give answers." Since the so-called Coase theorem is based on zero transaction costs, the conclusions reached using the theorem are misleading
and incomplete.

Frank Dietz and Jan van der Straaten (1992) discuss the missing links between theory and policy. Focusing on the externality theory, they point out that the most commonly used policy instruments focus on permits. Gregory Hayden (1993) calls for "Changing the Ideological Metaphor" by concentrating on the social institutions and the links between various aspects of society. In an article entitled "Economics and the Environment: Not Conflict but Symbiosis," the OECD (1984) indicates a mutual reinforcement between the economy and the environment and calls for an "integration of environment and economic policies." Don Taylor and Carleton Owen (1991) argue for improved stewardship of the forests as a means of sustaining future usefulness and protecting various habitats.[4] Even the Ecotourism Society has entered the fray by defining ecotourism as "responsible travel which concerns environments and sustains the well-being of local people" (Jones 1993, 7). Thomas Schelling (1992) discusses some of the issues involved with the global perspective of environmental problems: it may take a 2 percent decrease in GNP to avoid the global warming conflict.

However, unlike the older schools, these newer concerns do not describe specific instruments or remedies. Instead, they only indicate the problems. When remedies are prescribed, they tend to fall back on the old neoclassical (property rights) viewpoint of allowing the market system to do its work. In other words, the schemes are still exploitative in nature but are disguised as being environmentally friendly.

For example, Lisa Jones argues, "Unless local people come to view environmental conservation as economically profitable, we can kiss many of our unexploited wildlands goodbye" (1993, 7). This statement is fraught with contradiction. The danger of exploitation of these "wildlands" (presumably as pristine and primeval as the North American forests were prior to contact) is not due to the local, typically indigenous, people. Rather, the danger comes about from one of two avenues. Either large mining or timber companies are extracting the resources or the local social systems have been pushed out of the pre-contact equilibrium because of outside influences, thereby requiring the local economic subsystem to become exploitative and extractive. Another contradiction lies in the proposed uses of these "unexploited wildlands." To view ecotourism as a nonexploitative use is false. One only has to look as far as the national parks and wilderness areas in the United States to see how tourism can have harmful effects on the environment *and* the local population. Although ecotourism may be less damaging than open-pit mining, it is exploitative nonetheless. In short, the philosophy of exploitation, as shown above in connection with the doctrine of Manifest Destiny and the axioms of neoclassical economics, lies behind much of the literature concerning the economic *use* of the environment.

While the resulting policies have had some success in protecting or revitalizing aspects of the environment, degradation continues on many fronts. The evidence coming out of eastern Europe is disquieting at best. The problems began under earlier regimes but appear to be continuing if not worsening as these economies move toward market systems. As Boulding argued in 1966 and Dietz and van der Straaten voiced in 1992, a reformulation of the basic economic problem needs to be designed. As Hayden pointed out in 1993, a new *philosophy* of environmental issues needs to be developed.

COEVOLUTION THEORY

Richard Norgaard (1994 and elsewhere) has developed a body of thought based on "coevolution theory." The coevolution theory states that the various aspects of society coevolve in conjunction with the environment.

Although coevolution theory is essentially historical in nature because it cannot definitively predict the various natural or social mutations to come, it can determine some prescriptive remedies to obvious problems. Norgaard focuses on "ways of knowing" and "forms of social organization" when discussing the interaction between the environment and the economy. The severe discord among the social subsystems, or the deteriorating coevolution of the universe of man due to environmental damage, calls for new "ways of knowing" as well as new social organizations.

Hayden (1993) and Dietz and van der Straaten (1992), among others, call for changing the institutional aspects of environmental concerns. These new ways of organizing people, when further developed, may change the path of the system. However, as was evidenced by the proposed H.R. 1022, new ways of thinking also need to be formed. The return to the default assumption that progress is bound to happen if enough resources are thrown at the problem, as discussed by Ehrlich (1989) and presumed by Bailey (1993), has proven faulty.

TOWARD A NEW ENVIRONMENTAL SOCIETY

If we sell you our land, care for it as we have cared for it. Hold in your mind the memory of the land as it is when you receive it. Preserve the land and the air and the rivers for your children's children and love it as we have loved it. (Jeffers 1991, 23)

The idea of applying Native American ideals to the environment is certainly not new. As Calvin Martin (1981, 13) points out, "So it was in the heat and froth of the 1960s environmental movement, yet another title, 'ecological Indian'—was conferred on the idealized Native American, who was paraded out before an admiring throng and hailed as the high priest of the Ecology Cult."[5] Martin (1978) also argues that the Indian philosophy cannot be appropriate to the mainstream society because of a severe conflict between worldviews (as discussed by Trosper [1992]) and economic systems.

Others disagree. N. Scott Momaday argues, "I think that the Native American broad experience of the environment in the Americas is an important research resource for us. Native Americans need to be as informed (about pollution) as the rest of us, because they probably have more solutions" (1991, 437).

An example of what Momaday infers about environmental knowledge comes from the Hantavirus problem, which appeared in the spring of 1993. Peterson Zah (1993) reported that world specialists were lost as to the source of this deadly disease. Since many of the early deaths occurred on the Navajo Nation, traditional healers and elders were consulted by the Navajo government. Within days of consultation, the source of the virus was identified: deer mice. After two years of well-above average rainfall, the pinyon trees had yielded a bumper crop of nuts. This expanded food source caused an explosion in the mouse population. Since this was the only major change in the environment, the elders suggested testing the mice, and the source was found.

The mainstream and global economies are straining to find solutions to the environmental problems resulting from rapid and extensive industrial development. Can Native American ideals and philosophies be of use in this search? As Momaday stipulated, most likely.

Vine Deloria Jr. (1995, 57) argues that although mainstream science includes the idea of relativity, the practice of science and the use of science ignore the interdependence within the universe: "If scientists *really* believed in the unity and interrelatedness of all things, their emphasis would shift dramatically . . . and begin to deal seriously with the by-products of their experiments." He goes on to argue that Native American ideas, history, spirituality, and overall knowledge would be very useful in correcting obviously flawed hypotheses concerning the pre-contact Western Hemisphere.

The essence of the solution comes from our social compatibility theory. The problems are not simply environmental; rather, the problems stem from a disequilibrium between the various subsystems, namely, the economic and environmental subsystems. Countering Martin's concern over worldviews, Pirages (1977a), as noted above, pointed out that the mainstream society moved through significant changes as the economic subsystem developed. These changes are continuing at present as environmental issues are debated. The challenge is to develop structural compatibility between the various subsystems that allows for a sustainable economy within the closed environment or, to use Boulding's phrase, on "Spaceship Earth."

Within the mainstream economy, the environmental subsystem has been the duality of either exploiting a resource or leaving it alone. As discussed above, many pre-contact Native American societies maintained extensive and complex economies while living in harmony with the environment. The Native American environmental views did not ask the question of whether to exploit or not; rather, the question was how to live within the environment. This is the very question being asked by main-stream society today. Four examples show the distinction.

Nissenbaum and Shadle (1992) helped develop a land-use policy for the Puyallup Tribe in Washington State. After thoroughly consulting with the elders of the tribe and studying Puyallup culture and history, the authors drafted a policy with three interesting facets. First, any proposed land use must have no *net* degradation of the fisheries habitat. Second, the pro-posal must include a description of all environmental impacts. Third, preference will be given to proposals that increase the salmon population and enhance the fisheries. Compare the overall philosophy of the Puyallup Tribe with that of H.R. 1022, where no net loss of *economic activity* is the decision criteria.

The land-use policy is important because it offers alternatives to the usually mutually exclusive exploit or leave alone options. A particular land-use project could actually cause harm to a portion of the salmon fish-eries as long as it improved other sections of the habitat. The Puyallup culture involves the concept of stewardship for the salmon population. But this belief is not limited to a piece-by-piece protection of the fisheries; rather, the tribe seeks to protect the overall population, which may involve minor harm to specific locations.

Kat Anderson and Gary Paul Nabhan (1991) describe the difference between the two worldviews. The National Park system, in carrying out its mission, set aside the Organpipe Cactus National Monument in southern Arizona. Consequently, the Tohono O'Odam people were no longer allowed to harvest and manage the ecosystem, as they had been doing for years. Once the choice was made to protect instead of exploit—the only choices in the mainstream worldview—the ecosystem began to deteriorate. The Park Service returned to the original manage-ment practices of burning, flooding, transplanting, and seed sowing to save the "natural" ecosystem.

Plotkin (1993) describes various forest management practices among tribes living in the Amazon rain forest.[6] One of his examples is the vast difference in productivity between the agricultural plots of the natives and the settlers. The Native Americans use a multiculture approach, thus making their gardens difficult to discern from the surrounding forest. The settlers use a clear-cutting approach in their monoculture gardens. Of course, the multiculture approach is vastly more productive and is less susceptible to disease and pests.

Richardson relates how white trappers almost wiped out the beaver population in northern Quebec and Ontario in the 1930s after a railroad was built. By the early 1940s the provincial governments began to correct the problem:

For a change, aboriginals were involved in both schemes. In Quebec, once white trappers were excluded, traditional Indian methods were sufficient to restore the animals to the *levels that had existed for centuries*. The Quebec system was administered largely by the natives themselves. (1993, 137; emphasis added)

These examples of utilizing Native American practices, based on their environmental subsystems, result in more economic output and less degradation of the environment. Plotkin's overall work shows how the various subsystems can be developed to provide a growing and sustainable society with improved economic activity and sustained traditions.

After working with a particular rain forest tribe for over a decade, Plotkin provided the tribe a plant medicine handbook in the local language. He also helped develop a profit-sharing and investment strategy with several international pharmaceutical companies for continued research. One result of all this has been a shaman apprenticeship program for several tribes where no apprentices were previously in training. He concludes,

I feel strongly that this effort has helped validate their culture in the eyes of the Indians. Prior to this work, the Tiroe had only one book written in their language, the holy Bible. This research constitutes a true partnership between Western and Indian cultures; both share in any potential material benefits, but more important, this approach to ethnobotany helps the indigenous peoples understand the potential global importance of a fundamental aspect of their culture. (1993, 287)

Thus Plotkin shows how the ideas in this chapter can be put into practice: economic development and a Native American environmental view can work together to provide a vibrant and developing society. The global society can be enhanced by this development if the subsystems are allowed to reach a higher level of equilibrium.

All societies are coevolving systems searching for structural compatibility. Although it cannot be said of today's Native Americans, pre-contact Native American societies had vibrant economies working in conjunction with a healthy environmental subsystem. Societies begin to deteriorate when the compatibility between subsystems is disrupted, which can lead to a spiraling down instead of societal growth. The mainstream society is facing this type of disruption due to increasing environmental problems. At present, much of the work within the wide realm of environmental economics either treats the two subsystems as combative—exploit or leave alone—or as a simple matter of accurately identifying the costs and benefits. Although recent work, Hayden (1993) and Dietz and van der Straaten (1992), for example, have focused on institutional changes and systemic compatibility, much work remains to be completed in designing the institutions and understanding the systemic linkages. As Momaday

(1991) indicated, much can be learned from understanding Native American institutions and systems of social interaction with the environment.

NOTES

1. Anderson and Nabhan 1991. See also Horn and Hawkins 1991; MacLiesh 1991; and Josephy 1992.

2. Other reasons include population growth, drug abuse, failure of education systems, family makeup, and the like. As discussed below, all subsystems eventually reach a point of equilibrium (though not necessarily an optimal one). These other issues are well beyond the scope of the current discussion.

3. See Daly 1977, for example.

4. Both authors are executives for a large forest products company.

5. See Martin 1978, 157 for an earlier discussion.

6. See Smith 1994d for a discussion of the economic implications of Plotkin's work.

PART TWO

EXAMPLES
AND ISSUES

The remaining chapters of this book explain how the theoretical framework can be put into action. The more technical and practical chapters are formulated to allow for specific plans.

8

Managing Tribal Assets: Developing Long-Term Strategic Plans

As Native American tribes move toward self-determined governments and self-sufficient peoples, they face daunting problems.[1] Beginning from a status quo that includes unemployment rates ranging as high as 90 percent, concomitant social and health issues unseen elsewhere in the United States, and limited financial assets, tribes find need to develop long-term strategic plans. However, traditional economic development models and techniques are of little use in designing these plans. The National Executive Education Program for Native American Leadership (NEEPNAL) in conjunction with the Center for American Indian Economic Development (CAIED) has developed a method for aiding tribes develop such plans. Additionally, some tribes are earning substantial financial assets through gaming operations. Although these funds change one term of the development equation, the rest of the equation remains the same. These tribes still face the challenge of using their assets to build vibrant communities after years of destitution. Clearly, a long-term strategic community development plan is called for.

Traditional economic development tools such as economic base and location quotients are of little use in determining the future path of tribal societies, for several reasons. First, traditional tools are useful for communities already evidencing sustaining economies; however, when the local economy faces exorbitant unemployment rates and the vast majority of actual employment occurs in the governmental sector, any initial inventory of the economic base is essentially useless.

Second, the extreme social and health issues typically present lie beyond the scope of the usual economic analysis method. Any long-term development plan needs to address the broad spectrum of community development issues: health, education, substance abuse, crime, and myriad other social issues.

Third, all development projects need to be analyzed from both economic and cultural perspectives. Often traditional development plans have been misdirected due to what has been called "'the self-reference criterion'; the unconscious reference to one's own cultural values" (Deresky 1997, 76). When tribal development plans are conceived externally by members of the dominant culture, no matter how good their intentions, they tend to reflect the beliefs, aspirations, and values of their authors, rather than the ones espoused by tribal cultures. As tribes approach true self-determination, maintenance and renewal of traditional cultural values are at least as important as simple economic development. In many cases, seemingly profitable projects are deemed highly inappropriate for any number of cultural reasons.

Fourth and fifth, any tribal development strategy must take into account two (at least) levels of government not usually involved in development strategies. The tribal government is typically the only source of direct or indirect financial resources. For some tribes, the cultural aspects may point toward private enterprise; however, most individual tribal members have little chance of raising the necessary financial assets without commitments by the tribal government, either as a lender or as a guarantor. Alternatively, many tribes use tribal assets to operate tribally owned enterprises. In both cases, past, present, and future political issues need to be accounted for in any long-term plan. Historical and current interference in tribal activities by the federal government requires redress. The striking inconsistency of such interventions over time and across programs has resulted in heightened mistrust. On many reservations, various branches of the federal government, led by the Bureau of Indian Affairs (BIA), explicitly and implicitly oversee or control many resources available for development. Additionally, federal responsibilities to honor treaty obligations need to be accounted for in any long-term strategic plan.

Some final thoughts introduce the process. Morongo chairperson Mary Ann Andreas (1997) indicates the importance of tribes' determining their own goals and strategies: "No one knows the needs of our people like ourselves." Her goal has been to take tribal "taxusers and make them taxpayers." White Earth councilperson Erma Vizenor (1997), following Chairperson Andreas, indicated that "we are looking for ways to bring our people together with one mind, one spirit and one heart, but it is very difficult since we are so scattered." Five thousand tribal members live on the reservation and 20,000 live off the reservation. Councilperson Vizenor continued, "We need to come to our *own* tribal solutions to solve the problems in our communities." The process described below is a first step toward achieving the goals of these respected leaders.

COMMUNITY DEVELOPMENT: AN INTEGRATED APPROACH

For the sake of simplicity, the community makeup can be analyzed from six perspectives: economic, political, educational, social, cultural, and financial. This section discusses each one in turn.

The Economic Subsystem

Following our social compatibility theory, economic activity development cannot be analyzed in isolation. Instead, as will become clear, economic activity is best addressed last in the process! This may seem contradictory, since the most pressing issues for reservation communities are the lack of jobs and income. But the downward spiral of the overall society during the extended subsistence-level reservation period presents challenges more complex than merely attracting jobs to the reservations.

Economic activity is simply a means to the end of creating a healthy, vibrant community, and various options need to be compared. Three potentially competing outcomes are desired: an increased number of jobs, increased personal income levels, and increased tribal revenues via prof its. To further complicate the issue, profitability must be viewed from an economic perspective instead of an accounting one.

Any economic activities to be undertaken must show promise of prof-itability. Scarce resources cannot be devoted to job creation, for instance, if the enterprise does not show the prospect of sustainability. However, the concept of sustainability differs from a simple profit-and-loss accounting statement.

Consider a tribe currently spending $50,000 on various social welfare expenses. A projected tribal enterprise will provide employment for the people receiving the tribal transfers but will result in an accounting loss of $10,000. Keeping the example simplistic, if the earnings from employ-ment make the employees at least as well-off as before, this enterprise is profitable from the tribe's perspective. Although a private business could not sustain an annual loss of $10,000, the tribe realizes a $40,000 savings in overall expenses. Combine this with the social consequences of the tribal members earning their own incomes, and this enterprise is viable from the tribe's perspective. This is particularly true if the enterprise shows promise of future growth.

The triad of jobs, income, and profits holds potential conflicts. Consider a tribe with three investment options. The first is an agricultural enter-prise with the prospect of employing fifty people at $5 per hour. The agri-cultural enterprise will be sustaining, but it will not provide substantial profit for the tribal coffers. The second enterprise is a capital-intensive manufacturing enterprise. After training, ten people will be able to earn $20 per hour. This wage will be necessary to avoid a "brain drain" of the newly trained tribal members to border towns. Like the agricultural enterprise, the manufacturing plant will be sustaining but not particularly profitable. The third enterprise is a middle ground from an employment perspective, say, twenty-five employees earning $8 per hour. The third enterprise is a strong export business, such as gaming, and will earn the tribe substantial profits.

Developing a long-term strategic plan involves identifying the specifics of these three potential enterprises. However, the final decision *cannot* be identified from a simple economic or accounting perspective. Rather, the overall vision of the tribe in conjunction with the other subsystems has to be analyzed, and then only the tribal leadership can make the final decision.

The Political Subsystem

The governance structure of the local community dictates the direction of development planning. As discussed above, reorganization of the governance structure is beyond the scope of the activities discussed in this chapter. However, the existing structure has to be known. For example, some tribes support private entrepreneurial activity by providing site leases and such. On other reservations, the main focus is tribal enterprises.[2] Some tribes maintain a strong separation between economic and political activities but others do not. These issues, well discussed in Cornell and Kalt (1992a), help direct the focus of the strategic planning process.

The political subsystem of any society makes the rules. With regard to the First Nations, the political system can be very complex. The formal tribal government structure, often based on an IRA (Indian Reorganization Act) constitution, is only the first level of the complexity. Many traditional decision-making processes underlie the formal structure. As detailed by Cornell and Kalt (1992a), in many instances informal traditional structures conflict with the formal ones.

In addition to the internal structures, interaction between the tribal structure and the external structures of federal and state governments further complicates the situation. The issues of sovereignty are exacerbated when government-to-government relations are taken into account.

In order to design an effective community strategic plan, it is imperative to understand formal and informal political interactions. As discussed below, much of this information can only be gleaned through extensive interviews of tribal members.

The Educational Subsystem

Obviously, the viability of a long-term strategic plan rests on future workforce and social conditions. Therefore, an analysis of the educational system is imperative. Some reservations have BIA schools, others have 638 contract schools, and yet others use border town schools. The quality of the educational experience, which includes both the traditional skill orientation and cultural sensitivity, differs widely among these schools. Educational focus varies significantly between emphasis on dominant-culture language and skills and traditional tribal languages and skills. Language and cultural programs feed into the other subsystems.

The purpose of the strategic planning process is to develop the community with regard to the social compatibility theory discussed above. The vital importance of the educational system—both formal and informal—in terms of continuing the cultural heritage must be addressed. As tribes increase their control over their education programs and increase the number of well-educated tribal members, they will be able to make better self-determined decisions and therefore increase their de facto level of sovereignty.

For example, scholarship programs can be tailored to match the future needs of the tribe. Given limited resources, a tribe may set up the scholarship program to favor particular skills such as range management or horticulture. For many years, law school has been the destination of the "best and the brightest," but as reservations develop and gain true sovereignty, other skills can be targeted via selective scholarship programs.

The Social Subsystem

For simplicity, this is a catch-all subsystem including social issues such as elder care, day care, health care, substance abuse, spousal and child abuse, criminal justice, and recreation. Clearly some items in this list overlap elsewhere. Understanding the current situation and designing programs for the future are important aspects of the long-term strategic plan.

For example, in a Harvard Project on American Indian Economic Development paper entitled *Fort Belknap's Community Development Plan: A Teaching Case Study in Tribal Management*, which I coauthored with Jon Ozmun (1994), we discuss a plan by the Fort Belknap Indian Community that is based on a substance abuse center. The focus was determined by the tribal council, which saw unemployment and substance abuse as the two most pressing issues on the reservation. Commingling employment with a substance abuse program and the criminal justice system led to an integrated plan of action. This plan is discussed in detail in chapter 10.

Other examples include identifying the lack of day care opportunities as a major deterrent to employment, organizing a community cleanup competition, expanding the health care facility, sponsoring a tribal softball team, and the like. A healthy and vibrant community requires more than just jobs; identifying and addressing social issues is an important part of any strategic plan.

The Cultural Subsystem

The guiding force for all aspects of the strategic plan is the specific culture of the people. A plan for the Hualapai people would be very different from one for the Oglala Sioux people—even if they traded reservations. Since the purpose of any strategic plan is to improve the community and lives of the local population, all aspects of the resultant plan must be suitable for and guided by the cultural subsystem.

Culture is the way of living developed and transmitted by a group of people to subsequent generations (Harris and Moran 1991). Included in culture are artifacts, beliefs, ethics, moral and other values, and underlying assumptions that allow people to make sense of themselves and their environment. Culture is, as Geert Hofstede has said, "the software of the human mind" (1992, 12). As such, the cultural subsystem may be the most complex and difficult to analyze. Outside consultants, such as the author, may not be privy to many important aspects of the tribal culture. Certain taboos may not be broached, certain concerns may not be voiced, even certain names may not be spoken regardless of how extensive the interview process is.

An extended time period may be required for outside consultants to earn the confidence of people, and even then the outsider may not understand the subtleties of certain cultural mores. These problems are exacerbated when more than one tribe is represented on a reservation, such as the Fort Belknap or Colorado River Indian Tribes.[3] For these reasons, the process described below does not dictate or prescribe any plan of action. Only the tribal leadership can complete the final analysis.

An understanding of the cultural subsystem guides the process. Identifying certain sacred sites is vital. Certain cultural taboos make various types of activity objectionable on the surface. For example, if mining is viewed as a desecration of Mother Earth, then investigating mineral deposit potential is pointless. Furthermore, consultants who suggest that mining be investigated or pursued as a tribal enterprise will be insulting the members of the tribe and will lose their trust, without any other words being spoken. Additional suggestions by the same outsiders may also be viewed negatively after such a cultural misunderstanding.

Beyond setting parameters for the strategic plan, the cultural subsystem needs to be addressed within the plan. Formal and informal language programs can be designed. Merging the elder program with the day care program provides opportunities for sharing oral traditions. Developing suitable arts and crafts programs can sustain and expand cultural traditions. Artifacts, as the tangible examples of traditional culture, enhance interest in the less tangible cultural dimensions—the stories, legends, beliefs, and values of the tribe. Revitalizing traditional feast days and ceremonies can also become a tribal activity.[4]

The Financial Subsystem

Advancing the previously discussed subsystems requires financial assets. Investment in tribal enterprises, a tribal loan program for entrepreneurs, language programs, community cleanup days, and the like requires financial resources. Since most tribal members have few financial assets, these must come from the tribal coffers either through direct investment or via debt obligations.

For obvious reasons, many tribes will be wary about letting outside consultants have specific information concerning tribal finances. *This need not be a deterrent to successfully developing a plan.* NEEPNAL/CAIED staff members having only rudimentary knowledge of tribal finances have successfully employed the process described below. Since the tribal leadership makes the final decisions and actions, specific financial information is not necessary in developing the menu of opportunities.

Once again, this subsystem is a two-sided coin. Apart from working within the existing structure, the strategic plan needs to look for development opportunities. For example, an opportunity might exist for a micro-lending program for entrepreneurs to finance inventories or equipment repair. On a larger scale, a program might be arranged between the tribe and a financial institution circumventing the collateral and jurisdictional issues, thereby allowing tribal members to obtain larger loans.

Summary

Viewing the community development process through the lens of the social compatibility theory allows for an integrated approach. Using a simplistic listing of the economic, political, educational, social, cultural, and financial subsystems provides for a better understanding of the overall community. Once the existing situation is understood, development options can be introduced into the plan.

Recognizing the interactions among the subsystems is vitally important. Building a vendor village for the sale of arts and crafts to tourists may look profitable from an economic perspective. Then too expansion of the arts and crafts manufacturing sector may be important within a cultural perspective, since traditional methods can be handed down from the elders to the youth. The potential income from the sale of arts and crafts items may be seen as leading to renewed self-image and thereby reducing many social ills such as substance abuse. Thus an investment in a vendor village may look like a positive plan on many levels. But if the overall plan makes no allowance for individual artisans to obtain loans for an initial inventory of inputs, such as gems and silver, then the overall plan will fail.

THE PROCESS

The process of formalizing a long-term strategic community development plan is at once complex and simplistic. Similarly, it is both purposeful and improvisational. Obviously, since each reservation community is unique, there is no "one size fits all" strategy—either for the process or for the end result.

Interviews

The most important undertaking within the overall process is that of interviewing. This is particularly important for outside consultants. The interviews need to have an overall structure but must also be free-form in nature. It should also be expected that some people will have to be interviewed recursively. The interviews should be conducted in person in a location the interviewee finds comfortable. For instance, do not bring a high school student into the tribal chairperson's office! The time schedule should be loose enough to allow an expected half-hour interview to last an hour or more.

Having been invited to begin a strategic plan, the analyst should expect to spend several hours discussing initial ideas with the tribal representative in charge of the plan.[5] This may be the tribal planner or a council member. Beginning with broad strokes, focus on the current problems and projects. It is essential to determine the existing situation and plans. A good starting point is the Overall Economic Development Plan (OEDP). This will include at least a partial listing of existing and planned economic activity.

As details begin to come forth, focus on individual enterprises or activities. For the most part, the initial focus will be on economic activity. A tour of the reservation and selected facilities is recommended.[6] Since this is the lead person representing the tribe, she or he will also have strong ideas concerning directions for future activities. For example, a vendor village may be one idea. Once an initial understanding of the current situation and possible future activities is garnered, a series of interviews should be scheduled with other individuals.

Although it may not be necessary or possible to meet all council members, the council members themselves may request it. As mentioned, understanding the political climate is important. If it becomes clear that distinct factions exist on the council or within the tribal population, it is important to get all sides of the story. Council members can provide vital information on legal and intergovernmental issues and relationships.

Program administrators are another important source of information. Whereas council members have a political perspective, administrators have a "frontline" vantage point. Possible interviewees include the directors of the education, health, fish and wildlife, and other programs, the police chief, the tribal archaeologist, the director of the museum, and the managers of tribal enterprises. It should be expected that issues overlooked or ignored by the council members may be vitally important to these people.

Another important category of people to interview is the elders. Identifying respected elders and deferentially requesting insight into their knowledge is an important aspect of the process. These interviews can help focus the resulting plan on culturally sensitive issues. Elders can provide insights into the traditional culture and at the same time may be closely in tune with areas of friction between tribal values and values inherent in development plans. The council and the planner may be mostly motivated by the triad of jobs, income, and profit, whereas the elders may point out some issues that are culturally problematic. As mentioned above, an outside consultant needs to be patient to gain enough respect for some elders to be forthright.

The other end of the demographic spectrum, youth, should also be interviewed. College students and high school students provide a different perspective. The school or tribal library are locations to meet students.

As the interviews progress, certain names may become familiar or suggestions may be made. The interviews can include randomly selected ordinary private citizens, for example, people who work both on and off the reservation, single mothers, and parents at a basketball game. These are the people for whom the strategic plan is being developed—those who live on the reservation and face day-to-day issues. Their inclusion is vital to the general success of any development plan.

Regardless of who is being interviewed, a rough structure should be followed based on four simple questions. First, what is good about the reservation today? Second, what is wrong with the reservation today? Third, what would you like to see on the reservation in five, ten, and twenty years? Last, what would you *not* like to see in five, ten, and twenty years? The last question is very important from a cultural perspective, since the answers may point toward hitherto unknown taboos.

Depending on the circumstances of the planning process (e.g., travel), the interviews will take several days and may occur over a span of several weeks. As already mentioned, the interviews may be recursive in that some people may be interviewed repeatedly.

Although copious notes should be made during the interview process, the final report does not indicate the specific sources of any information. Assuring a level of anonymity allows the interviewees to be more forthright. This is especially important in small communities, where minor details of an interview can identify the interviewee to other members of the tribal community.

Secondary Research

Obviously, one phase of the project involves secondary research. From U.S. Census data to tribal reports to anthropological studies, this secondary research should be as exhaustive as possible. This research should also be cognizant of measurement and collection problems and biases in the data. For example, I researched soil salinization for one strategic plan.

Fortunately (though for the wrong motives), most reservations have been studied extensively in terms of natural resources. Tribal offices are typically repositories of dusty reports bursting from boxes and file cabinets. Certainly, modern analysis methodologies can supplement the older studies. Other information may be more problematic, for example, the fuzziness of unemployment rates on reservations. For the very reasons that processes like economic base and location quotient are infeasible, the process described here is only loosely scientific in nature. But the more hard data one can obtain, the better the resulting understanding of the existing circumstances and the potentials for development.

The Workshop

Following an initial round of interviews and extensive secondary research, a workshop is provided for tribal representatives. Scheduled for two to three hours, preferably with coffee and donuts, NEEPNAL/CAIED staff present an initial outline for a strategic plan.

Arriving with an overhead projector, a set of slides, and a "flipchart" tablet and easel, the research staff presents an overview of the project. Not all attendees will have been interviewed previously. Following the cyclical development model, the staff provides a loose plan of action. The purpose of the examples, which are developed from the previous research, is not to dictate what must be import replaced. Rather, examples are used to allow the audience to focus on the process of economic development.

Once the formal presentation is completed, the staff facilitates an open discussion based on the same four basic questions used in the interviews. This may be the very first time the director of the education program, the director of the museum, and the police chief discuss strategic issues instead of specific problems. When possible, one staff member facilitates the discussion and a second records thoughts and ideas on the flipchart tablet.

Other topics are garnered from the previous interviews, for example, various sacred sites needing protection or the success of the language program in the elementary school.

This record of the discussion is then added to the previous research notes and data for further analysis. It also becomes a permanent record of the event, and a transcription should be included in the report as an appendix.

Apart from the main purpose for the workshop, a secondary benefit may obtain. A regular formal strategic planning session may become part of the tribal schedule. On a quarterly basis, say, a similar meeting can be held to focus on the larger issues.

CREATING THE VISION

Following a second round of interviews, the workshop, and completion of the secondary research, a vision for the future needs to be formulated. This statement must be realistic yet optimistic.

Beginning with the initial conditions and based on the various answers to the future-looking interview questions, you need to distill the information into a straightforward, brief vision statement for the tribe. The vision statement needs to include accomplishments, for example, the high school dropout rate and unemployment rate will be reduced by more than half. The vision statement should be inclusive of the various subsystems discussed above, without being overly technical or academic.

The vision statement sets reasonable, though optimistic, targets for the development of the strategic plan. In mathematical terms, it sets the terminal conditions. The planning process then becomes a complex optimal control problem: given the initial and terminal conditions, what strategies will take the tribe from one to the other? After an initial draft of the vision statement is completed, several tribal representatives should review it for modification.

CREATING THE MENU

At this point several possible activities have been identified for each of several categories. For example, the categories may be tribal enterprises, private enterprises, community projects, education projects, health care issues, and governance modifications. The tribal enterprises category specifically identifies projects such as a motel, an RV park, a grocery store, a cattle ranch, the expansion of a forestry products plant, and a canning plant. All the various projects should be listed in an itemized outline.

In a purposely randomized order, each of the possible projects within a category on the list is discussed in the report. Unless they are obvious, no normative recommendations are included in the report. Instead, the benefits, potential problems, and conflicts and interactions with other projects are discussed. The last issue is of vital importance, since the integration of the several subsystems is the driving force behind the strategic plan. As already noted, leaving out one piece of the puzzle may lead to failure.

The detailed report should read like a menu. Some projects may be mutually exclusive for financial or other reasons, whereas others complement each other. The linkages should be indicated. Once the report is completed, it is forwarded to the tribal council or representative for further action.

CONCLUSION

The process described herein has been successfully (at least seemingly so) completed for various NEEPNAL/CAIED partner tribes. Having received the finished report, the tribal governments then determine which projects to pursue. At this point detailed business plans are developed for the economic activities to evaluate the specific feasibility of those projects. Similar plans and budgets are prepared for the nonbusiness activities. Then the process moves to the action phase, and the selected projects are actually undertaken.

The end result of the strategic planning process is therefore only the initial step on the path toward self-sufficiency and self-determination, but it is a vital step. In order to take this step, the tribal community must be looking forward and must be ready to take the risks necessary to reach into the future. Creating the vision of what that future may hold is more important, perhaps, than detailing the specific activities to undertake. The economic, community, cultural, and other endeavors within the body of the plan are simply the means to the end of reaching the vision of the people.

NOTES

1. This chapter is largely based on Anderson and Smith 1999.

2. Stephen Cornell and Joseph Kalt (1992a) discuss the compatibility between enterprise form, governance structure, and the underlying culture.

3. Assiniboine and Gros Ventre, and Chemehuevi, Mohave, Hopi, and Navajo, respectively.

4. Refer to chapters 5–6 for details on how cultural aspects can work hand in hand with economic development.

5. Be aware that the lead representative is likely to have other duties besides being interviewed for two days.

6. Have the tribal representative drive to facilitate note taking.

9

♨

An Example:
The Rosebud Sioux Tribe

In the previous chapters I addressed the problems facing reservation communities and some possible solutions. In the next two chapters I discuss possible development plans for specific reservations. I consider additional specific development issues following these exemplars.[1]

The difficulties facing reservation economies may reach a pinnacle on the Rosebud Sioux Reservation in South Dakota.[2] Adam Diamant (1988) conducted a detailed study focusing on possible enterprises that the tribe or tribal members might undertake as a method of economic development. However, this study was not particularly optimistic about the potential success of the development. Using Diamant's discussion of the Rosebud Reservation as an exemplar for other reservations, in this chapter I first provide a descriptive overview of demographic data of the reservation, and then I simply present an overview of Diamant's suggested activities. Using this list of possible outlets for prosperity, I conclude this chapter by arguing that a consolidated development plan could lead to the envisioned economic development within the confines of cultural and sovereign integrity.

Data from the 1990 Census on Housing and Population show some important distinctions between the Rosebud Sioux Reservation and both South Dakota and the United States as a whole. Rosebud has a population of 8,352, which is almost exactly 50 percent male and 50 percent female (4,132 male vs. 4,220 female). This compares to 51.2 percent female for the United States as a whole and 50.8 percent for South Dakota. Table 9.1 shows the comparative age distributions for Rosebud, South Dakota, and the United States.

Table 9.1 Comparative Age Distribution

Age	Total	Rosebud, %	South Dakota, %	United States, %
Under 5	1,154	13.8	7.8	7.2
5–17	2,613	31.3	20.7	18.2
18–20	408	4.9	4.5	4.7
21–24	469	5.6	5.3	6.0
25–44	2,180	26.1	29.4	32.5
45–54	564	6.8	9.0	10.1
55–59	256	3.1	4.2	4.2
60–64	233	2.8	4.4	4.3
65 and up	475	5.7	14.7	12.6

Source: 1990 U.S. Census of Population and Housing, STF 1A.

The most glaring result of this comparison is the large percentage of the reservation population under the age of eighteen. Experience in Indian Country leads me to explain this result as follows. First, poor nutrition, social problems, and health care in past years have lowered the life expectancy of Native Americans as a whole, and therefore there are comparatively few elders on the reservation. Compounding this, and more important in terms of economic development plans, is the fact that improving health care and altering social problems have significantly increased the number of successful pregnancies and the number of teenage pregnancies, which has increased the number of children and the percentage of children. Regardless of the causes for this shift in the age distribution, over 45 percent of the reservation population is school-age. The socioeconomic problems present on the reservation will become more problematic as this cohort enters their working years unless economic development occurs.[3] These data accentuate the need for improved education programs detailed below.

The racial and family distributions are shown in table 9.2. Obviously, the reservation has a significantly higher proportion of Native Americans. However, the data also show a significant difference in the makeup of

Table 9.2 Comparative Race and Family Statistics

	Total	Rosebud, %	South Dakota, %	United States, %
Native Americans	6,883	82.4	7.3	0.8
Other races	1,469	17.6	92.7	99.2
Households[a]	2,210	100.0	100.0	100.0
Married families	935	42.3	58.9	55.1
Male-headed families	206	9.3	2.7	3.4
Female-headed families	635	28.7	8.0	11.6

[a]The remaining households are nonfamily households.
Source: 1990 U.S. Census of Population and Housing, STF 1A.

families. The percentage of single-parent families, both male and female headed, is higher than in South Dakota and the United States as a whole.

Table 9.3 shows proxy data with regard to standard of living. Owner-occupied housing and monthly rent on the reservation are both much lower than for the comparative populations. Additionally, there is a difference between housing costs for Native Americans and for whites. These differences can be used to infer differences in living standards.

These preliminary data all tend to point toward significant socioeconomic problems on the Rosebud Sioux Reservation. Although Rosebud may be considered one of the poorest reservations, these data are representative of many reservations when compared to nonreservation locations.

Diamant (1988) studied the Rosebud Sioux Tribe and came up with a variety of development ideas. The potential enterprises include expanding the Forest Products Enterprise by increasing the harvest of trees and expanding the scope of operations to include lumber processing for construction and picnic tables; developing a commercial fish hatchery to import replace currently imported hatchlings; and developing a new export product to improve the tourism gleaned from tourism-based fishing permits. Additionally, Diamant suggests that the tribe expand and develop its hunting permit sales through herd and range management. The game available includes elk, buffalo, and antelope herds, as well as deer and small game. This is seen as export expansion. High levels of geothermal power make it possible for the tribe to develop aquaculture and silvaculture enterprises to grow food products and saplings for both import replacing and export purposes. In addition to harvesting and utilizing the natural resources, Diamant discusses the development of a microelectronics plant and a garment manufacturing enterprise. Both of these enterprises could gain a comparative advantage due to Section 8(a) certification (a federal set-aside program for minority-owned businesses). He also emphasizes expanding the local arts and crafts industry in terms of both quality and quantity.

Diamant suggests a long-term goal of developing the tourism industry once the amenities and social conditions of the reservation have been

Table 9.3 Comparative Housing Costs

	Rosebud	South Dakota	United States
Average value, owner-occupied housing ($000)			
Native Americans	23.7	33.0	72.5
Whites	35.3	50.2	113.7
Average monthly rent			
Native Americans	$160	$263	$334
Whites	$124	$167	$429

Source: 1990 U.S. Census of Population and Housing, STF 1A.

improved. He also suggests, most importantly for our purposes, providing incentives for locally selling goods and services, namely, developing retail services on the reservation itself.

But how are these development plans to be successfully implemented, given the current economic status of the reservation? The following model provides a methodology for analyzing the development process.

Diamant concludes that nearly all of the proposed ventures are likely to be insufficient for the Rosebud Sioux to realize economic self-sufficiency. However, he fails to recognize two possible avenues for success. First, he treats each activity individually with no agglomerating factors existing between activities. Second, excepting tourism, he focuses on a rather short-term or static planning horizon. In this section I provide a new understanding of the proposed ventures as an integrated development plan.

Several of the opportunities suggested by Diamant can be viewed, in the development framework, as being purely import replacing. These include retail and construction. Developing these ventures accomplishes several steps necessary to develop the initialization of a cycle of vigorous growth.

First, the multiplier concept bears importance here. For instance, developing retail services for the local residents keeps import earnings on the reservation for at least one more round of local spending. Of course, this leads to local employment and additional income when additional retail services are available locally; this new local income is then captured within the multiplier process. In Indian Country, the term "buy Indian" does not apply to the 1910 federal set-aside law; it means encouraging reservation residents to patronize local retail shops.

In addition to the income multiplier, the employment multiplier comes into play. This is further advanced in conjunction with the advent of the other proposed enterprises. As those businesses increase local and export industries, local employment increases, which leads to increased local sales *if local retail opportunities have also increased.* However, if there is no increase in the retail sector, then the border towns experience the multiplier effect.

A third influence of increased retail activity on the reservation is more sociological than economic. Increased income and employment have positive influences on both employees' families and the local population as a whole.[4] Although retail employment is generally low-skill entry employment, it provides an introduction to general employment skills, which can be useful when the employee moves on to more advanced employment. Increased income provides incentives for other family and community members to actively consider searching for employment. However, this only benefits the tribe if other employment is available. Otherwise, the small increase in local employment can actually lead to conflict. Thus the direct import replacing activities advance the local economy *if it is merged with the development of other activities that include career ladder opportunities.*

Diamant also proposes developing expanded or new export industries, which include arts and crafts, hunting, fishing, microelectronics, and garments. Increasing export activity increases the earnings of imports. For example, increasing the sale of buffalo permits provides income for the tribe through additional license fees or profits and increased income for the employees of the expanded enterprise. This new income earns additional purchases of goods and services from the off-reservation economy. However, if a substantial percentage of these expanded purchases is made through the expanded retail sector mentioned above, then the multiplier effect once again kicks into action.

Diamant also suggests mixed-purpose activities. If timber is locally processed and both exported and import replaced, then a combination of the above developments is obtained. Local construction of domestic dwellings occurs, which can be paid for through the income effects of the multiplier effect and increased imports. This new secondary development leads to increased levels of the multiplier effect, which of course begins the second cycle of vigorous growth.

In isolation, any one of these activities is likely to fail as a profitable enterprise or result in sustained development on Rosebud, as concluded by Diamant; however, when taken as an integrated plan of action, the various factors work together to support each other as an agglomerating force. Initially, these agglomerating forces may be small or even nonexistent. For this reason, a true entrepreneurial spirit may be required to get the process started. This could be a tribal enterprise such as Apache Aerospace, in which the agglomerating forces become intertwined with economies of scope, or it may be a tribal member accepting the risk. Once the initial enterprise begins to grow and show promise, the agglomerating forces will grow as the tribe and tribal members begin to see the success. In addition, the likely time frame of each enterprise adds support to the integration idea.

The easiest enterprise to begin is the increased retail activity, whereas increasing timber activity is likely to take one to three years to get on-line. During this time, expansion in retail services is likely to be exploratory and slow. But by the time the expanded timber efforts begin to see signs of fruition, the retail sector should be prepared for expansion. The next phase is increasing lumber capacity and then construction capacity. As the local economy expands, the capacity of the retail sector can be expanded, and the cycle continues.

As the economy of the Rosebud Sioux Reservation develops, new ideas and possibilities will develop. In other words, the development model of vigorous growth continues as new services and products are developed. As the population becomes more skilled and interested in development, new and improved import replacing and export activities will develop.

For example, as the demand for higher skill levels and employment increases, there will be increased interest in education, which may also lead to an increased number of teachers, resulting in import replacement of non-Indian teachers. As interest in employment increases, there may be a concomitant breakdown of the supposed cultural avoidance of manufacturing activity. Following modern management and production techniques, manufacturing employment need not be tedious, repetitive assembly line–type work; rather, it can be interactive and productive.

Much more importantly, the improved socioeconomic structure of Rosebud Sioux society stemming from these employment and income-producing activities will lead to increased interest in the culture and history of the tribe among the younger generation. When the day-to-day problems of subsistence are solved, there is more time for understanding and listening to the elders' concerns and history. Thus the cultural integrity of the tribe is sustained and advanced.

As the economy of the reservation develops, the tribe increases its sovereign powers because dependency on the federal government is reduced. Further, as development progresses, tribal members will gain expertise and experience, thus reducing the tribe's reliance on outside technical assistance.

The labor force on Rosebud is representative of many reservations in that it is fairly uneducated and has little work history. Although the conditions on Rosebud are worse than on many other reservations, it continues to serve as our exemplar reservation.

The workforce is estimated at 5,000 enrolled tribal members with an average sixth-grade education. The unemployment rate is estimated at 86 percent (Diamant 1988). The present is not prosperous and the future is not promising from a short-run perspective: the only jobs that could be successfully created would be low-skill occupations with little room for advancement and continued low income levels. A long-run perspective, however, suggests that these entry-level jobs are just what is needed to start the development process.

The development process is just that: a process. Moving from the status quo of depression and poverty requires a growing economy to sustain the population, which in turn would allow the social and cultural aspects of the society to flourish. The proposed enterprises for the Rosebud Sioux call for little in the way of preexisting human capital levels. Yet all of them call for developing the human capital stock as time progresses.

Retail services provide entry-level jobs, which eventually lead to bookkeeping and inventory skills development, as well as other job skills required for running retail outlets. Employment in the retail sector is also likely to encourage entrepreneurship in the future, which is facilitated by on-the-job training and experience.

The forest management, herd and range management, fish hatchery, and aquaculture and silvaculture enterprises involve both entry-level jobs and native understanding and appreciation of the existing resources. The arts and crafts enterprise involves existing skills and interest in the development of those skills. The microelectronics and garment enterprises provide for entry-level positions in assembly and packaging. These entry-level jobs will provide the necessary experience and opportunities for further development as time passes, and, given the agglomerating factors among the enterprises, coincidental development of a group of activities could provide the initial force that leads toward a self-sustaining cycle of vigorous growth.

Two common concerns, which are two sides of the same coin, become important at this point in our discussion. First, Native American populations are often said to be uninterested in developing their economies into miniaturized versions of the mainstream economy due to the supposed loss of cultural integrity. Second, it is commonly envisioned that cultural norms keep Native American societies from developing their economies.

In the first case, nearly every tribal leader in the author's knowledge views economic development as being necessary for cultural maintenance and integrity.[5] This is because only when tribal members are self-sustaining can they be involved in sustaining their culture. As long as the individual's primary goal is to merely survive (or worse, to avoid reality through alcohol), then the cultural integrity and heritage of the tribe suffers. A typical understanding in Indian Country is that the tribe/extended family comes first, then immediate family, then self.[6] But this can only be realized when the self has something extra after obtaining nutrition and shelter. Therefore, I maintain that economic development is a tool to achieve cultural integrity and self-determination with tribal sovereignty. Recall President John Steele's 1992 comment: "when you wake up and realize that not only is today going to be like this, but tomorrow is going to be like yesterday also, it is easy to understand that you simply go out and get a bottle."

The second issue is a common argument for the trust relationship between the federal government and the tribes. The concern is that Native Americans are unable to adapt to unknown circumstances. Clearly, this argument is folly. Native Americans have continuously adapted since settling this continent. Robin Ridington provides a discussion of the Thule People and how they adapted to life in the Arctic in pre-Columbian times (1992, 42–43). And Peter Nabokov (1991) provides detailed exhibits of how Native American populations have adapted to ever-changing influences of the non-Indian populations. Robert White (1990) explains how economic development has led to an increased interest in traditional cultures and language as well as an adaptation of mainstream management styles (by both Indian and non-Indian managers) to fit into tribal decision-making systems. There is also an increased social pressure toward formal education.

The point is that economic development should be seen as a means to an end, and not an end in itself. Given the Native American understanding of an extended time horizon, once the opportunity for development is realized, the necessary steps will be taken. Thus entry-level jobs are not seen as dead-end jobs; rather, they are seen as a beginning if there is a concomitant expectation for future development.

Quick calculations based on the available numbers show that Rosebud has an unemployed population of approximately 4,300 people. Clearly, no single enterprise is likely to make a significant dent in the current situation. A major manufacturing plant employing as many as five hundred people, assuming the required skills are available, would just begin to reduce unemployment on the reservation. Of the projects suggested by Diamant, the largest would employ roughly fifty people. Combined, the enterprises may employ from two to three hundred people in the initial stages. Therefore, looking for a development activity that provides a panacea for the unemployment problem is likely to leave tribal leaders disappointed.

In the next chapter I expand Diamant's analysis to include more social aspects of development. The previous discussion of social theory and the interplay between culture and economic development allows for a more advanced understanding of the development process on the Fort Belknap Reservation.

NOTES

1. This chapter is based on Smith 1994a.

2. The Oglala Sioux Tribe at Pine Ridge may actually "win" this competition.

3. The statistics for Rosebud Sioux do not differ significantly from those for many other reservations. In related work, I studied eight other reservations across the country. In one case the distribution is only slightly shifted downward because of a large non-Indian retirement village on the reservation. The other reservations all show over 40 percent of the population being under eighteen.

4. This point holds true for the remaining enterprises. The multiplier effect also holds for this aspect.

5. These include tribal government leaders as well as business and religious leaders. It also includes tomorrow's prospective leaders: today's university students.

6. Depending on the tribe, the level of allegiance differs. The point is that the importance of "group" takes precedence. This viewpoint stems from the importance of past and future generations and the importance of Mother Earth.

10

A Further Example:
The Fort Belknap
Indian Community

If the Rosebud illustration provided an example of why a nonintegrated plan is likely to fail, the case of Fort Belknap provides an exemplar of a thoroughly integrated community action plan.[1] As I explained in chapter 8, Native American reservations need to look toward *community* development instead of simplistic *economic* development projects. This chapter presents a visionary plan developed by Donovan Archambault for the Fort Belknap Indian Community.

The Fort Belknap Indian Reservation in Montana was described by James Lopach, Margery Hunter Brown, and Richmond Crow (1990) as exhibiting "the reality of poverty." Indeed, the council passed a resolution in 1984 stipulating alcoholism and unemployment as the two most pressing problems on the reservation. However, the future looks bright for this small Indian Community because a new community development plan is being considered to address the economic, social, and psychological problems inherent within any community facing dire poverty.

Of course, recent literature on economic development focuses on community-based approaches as well as cultural approaches to Indian reservations, rural communities in general, or the development of less developed countries (LDCs).[2] The evolution of what were originally called enterprise zones and were labeled "empowerment zones" in President Bill Clinton's budget proposal for 1994 has followed the same type of change.[3] Clinton's proposals included more social development aspects than the original "let's get jobs into the inner city" idea.

Whereas many communities, Indian and otherwise, have developed extended plans for redeveloping deteriorating local economies, most plans fail to specifically target the social and cultural aspects of the community. Although creating jobs, refurbishing infrastructure (including buildings), and bringing in dollars will lead to improved social conditions, most of these plans do not include explicit social aspects.

For example, it is argued that the downtown revitalization projects in many towns and cities across the United States will provide jobs, modernize the infrastructure, bring customers back into the area, and result in improving social conditions as the neighborhood starts to grow.

In contrast, many communities develop social rehabilitation programs without considering simultaneous economic development needs. Examples of these are drug rehabilitation, job training, and literacy programs.

Although each type of program has merit in its own right, the lack of integration limits the potential success of each. The Fort Belknap community action plan, in contrast, fully integrates all aspects toward its goal of improving the community through economic, social, and cultural programs. As such, Fort Belknap's strategic plan has applications not only throughout Indian Country but also for many rural and small urban communities.

Douglass North (1988) and Rosa Gomez Dierks (1999) explain the importance of institutions in terms of economic development. North argues that efficient institutions can improve the viability of development programs. He also argues that the institutions must fit within the overall society. Stephen Cornell and Joseph Kalt (1992a) argue similarly. The question of institutional reform is advanced in chapter 11. Within this framework, the Fort Belknap strategic plan fits within a viable set of institutions.[4] Other tribal governments, as well as small rural communities, can develop similar institutions with regard to zoning and interactive programs.

THE FORT BELKNAP INDIAN COMMUNITY[5]

The reservation is home to people from the Gros Ventre and Assiniboine Tribes. The Fort Belknap Agency was established by statute in 1882, and the original boundaries were set out in 1887. The northern boundary is the Milk River in northern Montana (Lopach, Brown, and Crow 1990, 118). The agency is adjacent to the town of Harlem. The estimated reservation population is 2,508 (1990 Census on Housing and Population).

The Community currently operates a gas station/convenience store, a highway rest area for the State of Montana, including a museum and gift shop, a grocery store, a small manufacturing facility, and other small enterprises. Fort Belknap's main industry is agriculture, including both farming and ranching. An Indian Health Service (IHS) hospital is located on the reservation.

In 1984 the council passed a resolution stipulating alcoholism and unemployment as the two most important community problems. As evidence of this, records for 1989–1992 show 3,759 alcohol-related arrests made by the Fort Belknap Police Department alone. In 1992, approximately $450,000 was spent on alcohol and drug treatment for Community members. Alcoholism, as on many reservations, is not simply an adult male problem: many women and adolescents are also afflicted. An unemployment rate of 78–85 percent clearly indicates the second problem (Archambault 1992).[6]

Many alcohol-related arrests result in sentences that include a treatment period. Alcohol treatment occurs at off-reservation sites. These clinics are anywhere from one hundred to three hundred miles from the reservation.

During the late 1980s and early 1990s the community purchased three ranches bordering the reservation. These are functional ranches including water, electricity, and buildings. Each ranch needs renovation and further development. This work involves purchasing fence posts from off-reservation suppliers at a cost of $1.25–$3.75 per rail. Once this renovation is completed, the ranches will be run as profit-making enterprises.

On the southern edge of the reservation is a small timbered mountain range. Currently, the Community spends funds on thinning contracts and has a desire to reforest the mountains. The reforestation program is currently on hold due to a lack of funds.

The thinning process is also problematic. At present, the thinned timber is simply slash piled and burned. These are typically dead, young, or scrub trees. The method used to accomplish the thinning is to let contracts to individual Community members. These contracts usually include advance payment for working capital, but the funds are rarely used for this purpose. Rather, many contractors use the funds for personal purchases, including alcohol, and the jobs are not completed. As a result, the Community has to finish the job, which results in additional costs.

In 1991, the State of Montana funded a rest area on the reservation to serve travelers along Route 2. The Community hopes to use this facility as a trailhead for a variety of tourist activities, including guided tours, trail rides, and camping. These trails must be built.

The Community also hopes to use the ranches as tourist attractions. They can serve as trailheads and as base camps for hunting parties as well. Hunting for buffalo, prairie dogs, game birds, elk, and other game is available. All of these plans lead to future employment possibilities for a variety of skill levels.

THE DEVELOPMENT AND SOCIAL
COMPATIBILITY THEORIES REVISITED

The first stage of the cycle of growth involves an initial export industry earning imports (the development model is described in chapter 4). In Fort Belknap's case the "imports" are the alcohol treatment services for community members paid with IHS funds and the fence posts purchased from off-reservation suppliers for the ranches. The second stage, and one of primary importance in the current context, is the development of import-replacing industries within the local economy. In this stage, the economy begins to locally produce hitherto imported products. The third stage involves developing new and innovative products and production techniques during the import-replacing phase. The fourth stage encompasses developing these new techniques and products into new export industries, which provide increased or substitute import-earning income. At this stage, the process cycles: new import replacing takes place, which develops new products, which cultivates a new phase of exports. Thus a cycle of vigorous growth obtains.

Growth occurs from the import replacing and export development process in the presence of five interwoven factors. First, as import replacing occurs, the number and diversity of employment opportunities increase. Second, as employment earnings increase and the multiplier effect obtains, the region enlarges its import markets, providing imports of new and different kinds. Third, as activity and employment increase, jobs and activity spread outward from the city hub to the hinterlands, thereby increasing economic activity in the surrounding areas. Fourth, as the process continues, new uses for existing technology are found and new technological developments occur as entrepreneurial activity expands. And last, as the process proceeds and new businesses are opened, there will be an increase in the capital stock of the city region. These five forces of growth lead to increased economic activity and employment and lead toward the development of the cycling of growth: new exports earning increased and new imports. And the process cycles.

However, most problems at Fort Belknap and within other communities are not strictly economic ones. Fort Belknap and many Indian reservations face problems concomitant with high unemployment rates. Other communities face similar issues due to plant (military base) closings, farm failures, and the like.

In chapter 1 I presented a social compatibility theory based on the integration of various subsystems of society. Any development plan must address these other subsystems.

For the Fort Belknap Indian Community, the original shift involved the economic subsystem. Simply put, the transition from being hunting Indians of the plains, after many years of conflict and war, to a reservation—transfer—based economy severely shifted the economic subsystem. For reasons listed in chapter 3, the economy has not found any method of redevelopment. Thus the remaining subsystems have moved to a new equilibrium with the transfer-based economy. The results of this new equilibrium include high alcoholism rates, low education rates, spousal and child abuse, and a plethora of other social ills present in any severely economically depressed society. In short, a prosperous economy, or even a viable one, is not the *final goal* of Fort Belknap or any other economy. In other words, economic development is a necessary requirement for social development, but it is by no means a sufficient one.

Richard Norgaard (1988) argues, in a slightly different framework, that biological extinction occurs when there is a difference between adjustment rates. Norgaard argues that these differences lead to biological extinction when, for example, climate changes occur at a quicker rate than physiological adjustments. Alternatively, when the economy of a previously isolated population enters a global market, the economic adjustment may outpace the adjustments of a biologically diverse ecosystem. As the agriculture moves from multiculture to monoculture because of outside economic forces, some of the biodiversity is lost.

In the current context, Norgaard's theory can also be applied to the social framework. Differences in adjustment rates between the economic subsystem and other subsystems cause severe problems. The various social problems faced by the Fort Belknap Indian Community arguably have resulted from the difference in adjustment mechanisms when the economic system was altered by the reservation system.

Communities facing plant, sawmill, mine, or military base closings fear similar results. Severe social and cultural dislocations can occur when the main economic activity disappears, involving much more than the loss of paychecks. However, unlike Indian reservations, out-migration from these communities further exacerbates the problems for those remaining in town.

The strategy of developing an integrated community development plan is at once complex and simplistic. Jane Jacobs (1984) describes the *process* of stimulating sustained economic development. According to Barbara Ward (1962), this may not be sufficient to lead to overall social growth, but it is likely to be necessary. North (1988) argues that governmental institutions need to be structured to minimize the costs of transacting economic activity. In an article entitled "The Issue of Compatibility between Cultural Integrity, and Economic Development among Native American Tribes" (1994b), I employed a social theory to explain how institutions and economic projects must meet with cultural aspects of the indigenous people to be successful. I also argued that indigenous cultures can aid in the economic process. According to the social compatibility paradigm, a match between adjustment mechanisms or severe consequences may obtain.

THE FORT BELKNAP COMMUNITY ACTION PLAN

The community action plan stems from the 1984 council resolution identifying alcoholism and unemployment as the two most problematic issues on the reservation. With Jon Ozmun (1994), I detailed the evolution of the idea from its inception to the point when federal appropriations were made for a detailed feasibility study and the development of a plan of action. At this writing, the plan is merely that—a plan.

Beginning with the $450,000 of IHS funds *already* spent on alcohol treatment, two treatment centers will be supported by the Fort Belknap Indian Community. One will house and treat adult men and will be located on the ranch on the western border of the reservation. The second will house and treat adult women and adolescents on the ranch on the eastern border. Each clinic will be designed, initially, for 8-10 patients. The patients will primarily come from the criminal justice system: people arrested for alcohol-related crimes.

Each clinic will offer the usual treatment programs as well as "employment." Another facet involves traditional cultural aspects to allow the patients to gain a sense of purpose as members of the Gros Ventre and Assiniboine Tribes, as well as members of the community.

The payments for working will be made as a stipend. The patient will never actually have access to a cash payment. Instead, the stipend will be distributed to pay for various services. Portions will be used to *pay for the treatment process*, pay for travel expenses for family members to the center, support for family members through grocery store accounts, and personal items such as cigarettes and toiletries during treatment. Any residual balances upon graduation will revert to the centers' accounts.

Adult men will primarily work in physical labor positions. They will complete the thinning, fencing, cabin construction (for tourists and hunters), and trailblazing for the trail rides. Once the construction is completed, these patients will work as ranch hands and maintenance workers. Other positions will include cooks, cleaners, bookkeepers, and other auxiliary positions. This work will build working skills and self-esteem. Combined with the cultural aspects of the treatment, this program will lead to a much higher success rate than the current off-reservation treatment system.

Adult women and adolescents will work on other projects. The reforestation is not physically taxing and does not involve dangerous machinery.[7] This project will include collecting seeds, growing seedlings, and replanting seedlings. These patients will also work on the community farms and in a proposed greenhouse project.

The produce from the farms and the greenhouse will be "sold" to the schools, the hospital, and other community facilities. And the Community will use timber grown in the newly reforested areas for several purposes.

As the process proceeds, the patients will "graduate" to positions such as supervisors, herd managers and wranglers (cattle, horses, and buffalo), trail guides, secretaries, nurses aides at the hospital, and the like. As the success of the treatment plan proceeds, fewer and fewer patients will need treatment, so full-time jobs can be created as the ranches, tourist trade, hunting program, and greenhouse become productive. Also, patients can be "imported" from neighboring reservations and communities (i.e., the treatment service will become a new export). This will provide full-time jobs for the treatment center workers.

The stipends earned by the patients will be spent in community stores, thereby increasing sales and employment. Part of the income earned by the workers and "graduates" at the ranches and clinics will also be spent at the stores, thereby increasing the multiplier effects.

In order to prevent Community members from using the program for employment purposes, any recurrent problems will be treated using the existing off-reservation system. In other words, once a member has graduated from the program, a second arrest will result in off-reservation treatment. Members will only be eligible for treatment at the on-reservation clinics once every twelve months.

THE THEORETICAL FOUNDATION REVISITED ONCE AGAIN

The Fort Belknap community action plan includes almost all of the prescriptions included in both theories discussed above.[8] This section discusses how the plan fits into the combined theory. However, following the social compatibility theory, it is important to note that evaluation of the plan must be made in the broad context of *social development* and not simply from a financial one.

During the NEEPNAL (National Executive Education Program for Native American Leadership) conference with council members from the seven Montana reservations, an extended discussion took place concerning evaluation criteria for economic development projects. A consensus was reached that employment and social goals are at least as important as financial ones. As long as a project is self-sustaining in the long run, then the jobs it creates are a fundamental success. Furthermore, the concept of self-sustaining differs in this context. As discussed in chapter 8, for example, if a project is losing, say, $50,000 a year, but reduces tribal expenditures on transfer payments and administration costs by $60,000, then it is self-sustaining. The reduction of $10,000 in tribal expenditures combined with the new jobs indicates a project's success. As I pointed out in Smith and Ozmun 1994, part of the persuasion used in the funding process was the fact that improving alcohol treatment will reduce IHS expenditures on alcohol-related injuries and illnesses.

Combining the IHS money with the $10,000–15,000 spent on thinning contracts, an annual expenditure of at least $460,000 is available for the plan. In a sense, the Community is importing alcohol treatment from the off-reservation sites. The new on-reservation treatment sites will import replace the existing system.

In addition, instead of the thinning activity resulting in a bonfire, fence posts will be produced. Import replacing fence posts on the ranches and trails will further save Community funds.

The funds saved on thinning and fence posts can pay for renovations to the ranches and the construction of the trails. Since this work is very labor intensive, the work completed by the patients is an essential aspect of the plan. Without this resource, it is unlikely that the Community could pay for the labor required for renovation and construction.

The import-replacing facets of the plan lead directly to developing new exports and new import replacement. Without the savings and labor, the hunting and tourist activities would be delayed. Once these activities become profitable, the profits will finance the greenhouse project. The greenhouse will then import replace fresh produce within the Community, thus furthering the multiplier effects.

The interaction between social subsystems is also addressed by the plan. Currently, the treatment system involves a couple of hours each day in counseling and many hours of idle time at the treatment center. Specifically linking counseling with "employment" is aimed at improved success.

Donovan Archambault, the primary creator of the plan, understands the interaction between unemployment and alcoholism. "Let the adults, adolescents see each other sober and earning a living. Is this going to make a difference?" He believes so. "If you had something to look at and say I did that right there, maybe that would be an incentive to keep you sober."[9]

The improved cultural and visitation aspects of the plan also address the various subsystems. The off-reservation centers are designed for non-Indians, and the distance between the center and Fort Belknap discourages family visits. Additionally, the use of the stipends to help support the client's family provides a linkage. Finally, the fact that work is being accomplished for the betterment of the Community supports the linkage between self and Community identity, which is very important within Indian cultures.

Fort Belknap's community action plan contains all the aspects of the above prescription for vigorous growth, at least for the first cycle. It also recognizes the vital importance of integrating economic development with other areas of development within a society. Thus it should work—*at least in theory*. But what about in practice? The Fort Belknap Indian Community has received a $200,000 federal appropriation through the Department of Labor to complete a detailed feasibility study and plan of action to locate the alcohol treatment centers on the reservation. The feasibility study has not yet been completed and thus no conclusions are available as of this writing. However, the plan, as described, does include two problematic areas: postgraduation activities for the clients and the capital funding requirements.

Two issues are pertinent to postgraduation activities for the clients. First, most of the clients receive treatment as a requirement of a criminal sentence. The typical client serves a ninety-day sentence, with the first thirty days involving treatment. In the current system, the prisoner returns to jail for the remaining sixty days.[10] The problem arises with how this jail term interferes with the success of the program.

One solution would be to allow the prisoner to continue working in the program after treatment. The prisoner could be housed either on the ranch or in the jail. The work aspects would continue, but a problem develops with funding the stipend payments. The feasibility study and plan of action must address this issue.

The second problem area for program participants comes about with the postsentence time period. What employment opportunities, if any, will be available for the graduates? Clearly, if the plan is successful, employment opportunities on the reservation will be increasing, but if the full-time jobs are only open to program graduates, then a bizarre Murrayesque scenario occurs with people getting arrested and sentenced to gain access to the employment program.[11] The plan of action needs to specify the transition phase and employment procedures within the various enterprises.

The second fundamental difficulty with the plan is the required capital funding. The original budget shows the *treatment* plan to be self-funding. Profits from hunting permits and reduced expenditures on thinning contracts and fence posts are included in the budget. But the original figures do not include any capital expenditures for the cabins used by the hunters or any of the other required expenditures. The plan of action must identify the capital expenditures requirements and identify methods to access these funds.

CONCLUSION

Fort Belknap's community action plan addresses the two most pressing problems on the reservation: alcoholism and unemployment. Merging treatment with developing work skills and a work ethic should lead to greater success than is realized by the current system of off-reservation treatment. From a community development perspective, the plan is much more than simply linking the solutions. Indeed, it has the potential to lead the Fort Belknap Indian Community toward a cycle of vigorous societal growth. As such, the plan provides an exemplar for reservations and other depressed communities.

Although the plan has distinct advantages stemming from the communal nature of a reservation government, it also has applications to non-reservation communities. A city government may not be able to specifically link various aspects of a community development plan, as an Indian reservation can, but it can implement the integrating aspects of this plan. The importance of Fort Belknap's plan is the integrating characteristic. The plan addresses evolving economic activity and interweaves other social and cultural aspects into the fabric. As such, other communities can learn from their experience.

At this writing, the success of the community development plan, indeed the feasibility study, is unknown. The measurement of any success will only be available five to ten years after the plan is in place. Although the qualitative measurement may be rather difficult to evaluate, a precise measuring stick is quite simple. The original impetus for the plan was the 1984 council resolution. If the unemployment rate and the number of alcohol-related arrests decrease, then the plan can be deemed a success.

NOTES

1. This chapter is based on Smith and Ozmun 1994. For a detailed discussion of the political issues involved with the development plan, see Smith and Ozmun. The original two-part case was written as a teaching case for management, business policy, and economic development courses at the junior or senior level. Extended thanks are due Donovan Archambault for his friendship, insight, and willingness to sit up all night discussing these issues.

2. See, for example, Barkley 1993; Edgell 1992; Edwards 1983; and Perry and Dixon 1986.

3. See, for instance, DeMott 1993; and Glover and Brownridge 1993.

4. See Smith and Ozmun 1994 for details concerning the interagency aspects of the plan.

5. See Smith and Ozmun 1994 for a more detailed discussion of the evolution of the community action plan.

6. Readers concerned with funding procedures will be interested to know that the referenced proposal was the only documentation used to earn a $200,000 federal appropriation through the Department of Labor. The proposal is included in Smith and Ozmun 1994.

7. Federal labor statutes limit the types of machines that can be operated by young workers.

8. My original knowledge of the plan came during a workshop given by the National Executive Education Program for Native American Leadership (NEEP-NAL) for tribal council members in Missoula, Montana, in November 1993. During a blizzard in January 1994, I visited Fort Belknap to complete the primary research for this chapter.

9. Interviews, January 1994. See Smith and Ozmun 1994 for complete details on Donovan's philosophy concerning the plan.

10. Although the jail term may not actually occur. Unbelievably, the client is given a bus ticket to travel from the treatment center to the reservation!

11. See Murray 1984, 212–16 for a discussion of unintended rewards.

11

Developing Tribal Resources

In chapters 9–10 I presented discussions of proposed development plans on two northern plains reservations. In earlier chapters I provided an overview of the theoretical processes and potentials for development of Native American communities. In this chapter I change the perspective by introducing brief descriptions of some of the more technical details requiring attention during the development process.

Many other sources provide expanded details of the technical issues of capital funding, technical training, education, management, entrepreneurial development, enterprise boards, and institutional reform. Rather than repeat these other sources, this chapter introduces the importance of these aspects within the context of the development process.

CAPITAL FUNDING OPPORTUNITIES

Without delving into the historical difficulties of sovereignty and collateral, this section discusses possible avenues of successfully accomplishing the development and acquisition of capital funding and capital formation. While much research and policy discussion has centered on making capital funding available to Native American tribes and individuals, such funding is still a major deterrent to economic development.

Several possible types of enterprise have been offered as potentials for development. These are tribal enterprises either with or without outside ties, private enterprises either with or without outside ties, direct investment by outside firms, and sole proprietorship. Each of these has different characteristics in terms of raising the required capital funding. Direct investment is the easiest to discuss: if a contract providing a site lease to an outside firm is agreeable, then that firm will raise the capital funding on its own.

Tribal enterprises developed in partnership with an outside firm face the next easiest capital funding search. The outside firm either provides the funding or is able to cosign for loans. Further, Small Business Association (SBA) and Bureau of Indian Affairs (BIA) loan guarantees are available for a variety of ventures. Tribal enterprises developed independently face more difficulties in raising the necessary capital funding. In this case, it is vitally important that arrangements for default be expressly stipulated and adhered to. This may involve waiving the tribe's immunity rights and giving the lender the right to take temporary control of the facilities for the duration of a lease period. These two actions will make lenders much more willing to invest in Indian Country.

There is, however, a serious downside risk that has to be weighed when negotiating with outside agents. The history of Indian–white relations is full of scams and make-money-quick deals. It is very important that tribal representatives conduct an independent study of any prospective enterprise and check the background of the outside agents. One example of how things can go awry is the Nebraska Sioux Lean Beef enterprise. This joint venture between the Oglala Sioux Tribe and an outside investor was entered into hurriedly due to the potential loss of a HUD grant. The results of this enterprise were disastrous for the tribe (Jorgensen 1990a, 1990b).

Private enterprises can raise capital through the usual capital markets as well as through the SBA and the BIA. For example, SBA programs include 7(A) and 502 guarantees, and 504 loans. BIA programs include the Indian Revolving Loan Fund, the Indian Loan Guaranty Fund, and the Indian Business Development Grant Program. There are also the Business Consortium Fund for minority businesses and FmHA loan guarantees (Ramirez 1992).

Once again, tribal involvement in the process is required due to the trust nature of the land. In the case of BIA loan guarantees, an encumbrance of lease holdings must be processed by the tribe. This allows the lender to take control of the facility for the duration of the lease in the case of default. The SBA requires a subordination of lien rights to be processed by the tribe. This releases the lender from having to continue to pay lease payments on the land in the case of default (Mike 1992). The tribe must be willing to encourage development by providing these agreements.

Another potential method of making capital funding more readily available would be to design a system of regulations and negotiations between tribal members and outside lenders. During the business site lease application process, the tribe would act as a clearinghouse for the capital funding aspects of the process. Since the business site application and the funding solicitation application require detailed business plans, this would reduce the amount of regulation and paperwork for the entrepreneur. The tribe could either give tentative approval for the site lease, dependent on the acquisition of the requisite funding from the outside lender or vice versa. The benefit of this method would be that the tribe would work with the lending agent in the analysis of the feasibility and profitability of the business plan, thereby reducing redundant analysis. Also, the lending institution may be more prepared to provide technical analysis and recommendations, since this is its primary purpose, thereby reducing the need for government bureaucracy.

A second phase of the process removes the difficulties with jurisdiction, sovereignty, and trust status. Through negotiations between the tribe and the lending institution, the tribe would accept responsibility for being the debtor of last resort. Once the lending agent had followed all normal business practices in an attempt to receive payment on the loan, the loan would default to the tribe. At this time, the site lease and the collateral would revert to the tribe. This, of course, is stipulated in the site lease and loan agreements with the entrepreneur. Once the tribe has taken control of the property and site, it will attempt to find another tribal investor to take over the business. In essence, this idea is modeled after the way the IRS handles tax delinquencies.

Instead of BIA or SBA guarantees, the tribe is guaranteeing the loan. The total amount of capital funding available could be negotiated, depending on the financial resources of the tribe. This method has a twofold benefit. First, outside lenders would be more willing to make loans to on-reservation businesses because the difficulties with collateral and jurisdiction are alleviated, since the tribe is using its financial assets as collateral. As long as the contract between the lending institution and the tribe addresses the immunity issue, the lending agent benefits. The second benefit is the probable reduction in the interest rate on loans. Since the loan is guaranteed, the risk in the enterprise is moved from the lender to the tribe.

Robert White (1990) discusses three additional capital funding avenues. A private corporation, Tribal Assets Management, acts as a facilitator between tribes and venture capital markets. This corporation came about through negotiations on behalf of the Passamaquoddies. Since then, they have brokered negotiations for several tribes (White 1990, 49–50). A second potential funding source is issuing state industrial revenue bonds. The Mississippi Choctaw leased land to the city of Philadelphia, which then sold a bond issue (White 1990, 61). If a tribe is able to convince the local off-reservation border town of the benefits of employment, then similar arrangements can be made elsewhere. Third, the Confederated Tribes of the Warm Springs Reservation negotiated a loan wherein the sawmill would revert to the bank in the case of default for operational purposes until the resulting profits paid off the loan (White 1990, 205). This is much like the encumbrance of lease holdings required for BIA loan guarantees. All three of these opportunities for capital funding availability protect the sovereignty and communal land base of the tribe.

In any case, capital funding can be found if the project is well planned and well thought out. Technical assistance in developing business plans and the like can be sought from the organizations listed in Timeche (1992, 1995). The point is that capital funding is available for potentially profitable projects.[1] There may be additional requirements and paperwork for projects in Indian lands, but these protect the tribe's sovereignty and self-determination efforts. However, the tribe must be willing to accept some level of risk along with the outside lender.

TECHNICAL TRAINING

A major barrier to development in Indian Country is the lack of technical expertise. This shortage exists in terms of developing business plans, accounting systems, forest management, and the like. Another severe difficulty is the scores of accumulated planning documents that no tribal expert can read or put into action. In short, the combined cause of these difficulties is the shortage of timely and pertinent technical assistance.

Organizations such as the National Center for American Indian Enterprise and Development, the Center for American Indian Economic Development, and the First Nations Financial Project provide necessary and relevant technical assistance for problem-specific purposes. Combining these with SBA and BIA assistance, among other sources, opportunities to gain the required technical knowledge for economic activity exist. In short, technical assistance is available *if the enterprise knows how to access it.* This is another reason why the tribe may want to develop an economic development corporation and employ a technical assistance expert.

Another form of technical assistance is available through the Mentor-Protégé legislation (P.L. 101-510, sec. 831). This program links major defense contractors with small, disadvantaged businesses for technical assistance and other linkages (see Reed et al. 1991). This new legislation has great potential for tribal enterprises interested in subcontract work.

TRAINING AND EDUCATION

As with technical assistance, training is available through various sources. The Job Training and Partnership Act (JTPA) provides funds for preemployment and initial training of employees. State-run internships and private sector co-ops are available for college and university students. There are numerous tribal two- and four-year colleges across the country. Additionally, trade and vocational schools are available. These and other sources of education are subsidized at many levels. However, a compound problem arises when individuals finish their training.

A common problem is the "brain drain." A tribe's best and brightest young members gain advanced training, but when they attempt to return to their reservation, they find that their hard-earned skills are unneeded. Compounding this is the unavailability of qualified tribal members when the tribal enterprises are in need of an employee with advanced training. This issue is the focus of chapter 12.

A well-executed master plan for development could alleviate this problem. Much like the armed forces, tribes could determine future needs and then provide incentives for individuals to study in particular fields. For instance, if Rosebud decides to go ahead with the microelectronics enterprise, there will be a future need for electrical engineers and computer programmers. Given limited funds for tribal scholarships, the tribe could designate the requisite funds to students studying these particular fields before allowing students to choose any field of study. This type of matchmaking, combined with corresponding co-ops and internships, will lead to vigorous development on the reservation.

Two examples provide insight into the importance of guided training. The Navajo Nation and Northern Arizona University have negotiated a Memorandum of Understanding regarding a scholarship program. These scholarships are administered by NAU and target Navajo students in specific major fields of study such as accounting and finance. Similarly, NAU and the Fort McDowell Yavapai Indian Community have established the Wassaja Scholarship for students who will commit to completing a minimum sixty hours per semester of community service to an Indian community. The latter scholarship does not target specific majors but does require applicants to design their individual Indian-based community service programs.

MANAGEMENT

Each reservation is a unique economy facing problems particular to the setting and history of the tribe. However, reservations have similarities. As such, two possible methods of development are possible. First, privatization of enterprises can be stimulated by encouraging entrepreneurship through workshops and tribal programs.[2] The alternative method works through tribal enterprises.[3] This latter structure may be facilitated by the formation of an economic development corporation.[4] The question is, which of these two paths should the Rosebud Sioux or any other tribe follow? I address this question in detail below. Regardless of which method is used, many tribes have few individuals skilled in the various areas of management necessary for the proposed enterprises. Although many Indians are achieving college degrees, the dearth of skills is still apparent.

Thus management skills must come from off-reservation labor markets. This may be achieved in several ways. These include direct hiring by the tribe, joint ventures with off-reservation corporations, or attracting off-reservation businesses onto the reservation.

A tribal enterprise or a private business may be able to attract outside management specialists to manage the business. This may be particularly feasible if the enterprise has some unique product and an individual is interested in this particular opportunity. For instance, a silvaculture enterprise may interest an expert who is willing to undertake management of the sapling project. However, this presupposes that the tribe or private owner is able to formulate a detailed business plan under which the technical expert works.

A second alternative is a joint venture between the tribe or individual and some off-reservation business. Examples of this structure are Hopi Technologies, Tooh Dineh Enterprises, and Apache Aerospace in Arizona. The Mentor-Protégé legislation mentioned above provides added incentives for this type of venture. Adam Diamant mentions a relationship that once existed between IBM and Rosebud. In this case the outside organization provides the technical assistance and management assistance necessary to run the operation, but the actual plant is owned either by the tribe or a tribal member. In the case of the proposed microelectronics and garment plants on Rosebud, the outside firm would be the sole purchaser of the plant's output. An alternative would be profit sharing between the tribe and the outside firm. For instance, a forest products plant could sell to various buyers, but the partner firm would share in the profits or charge a consulting fee.

A third method of attracting the necessary management skills would be to attract outside firms to open branch plants on the reservation. This would require definitive leasing agreements stipulating the firm's use of tribal land and resources, as well as a stipulation for the tribe to purchase the facilities at some point in the future.

The current difficulties that the Navajo and Hopi Tribes are experiencing with the Peabody lease should act as an object lesson for this type of agreement. This long-term contract, signed in the 1960s and extending past the year 2000, was negotiated by the BIA and has become a point of contention for all parties involved. The exorbitant use of water to slurry coal from eastern Arizona to Nevada is lowering the level of the aquifer, but no stipulations were made in the contract for subsequent renegotiations or purchase of the facilities by the tribes (Masayesva 1991).

Regardless of the mix of management agreements used in developing the proposed activities, there also needs to be a formal stipulation that tribal members will be trained and accepted as managers in the future. This could include on-the-job training for less complex management functions such as bookkeeping and inventory control. It should also include scholarship funds to send students to college, university, and trade school. This long-run approach is necessary to provide for self-management in the future.

Miriam Jorgensen (1990a, 1990b) has described the failed Sioux Lean

Beef enterprise of the Oglala Sioux. However, the agreement between the tribe and the outside investor did include employment and training criteria. Had the outside investor honorably led the business toward success, these criteria would have been as important as the potential profits.

ENTREPRENUERSHIP

For reasons of culture and severe dependency, it has been argued that the concept of entrepreneurship is not pervasive in Native American societies.[5] Also, given the low levels of savings by reservation populations, there is little available private capital for the few individuals interested in opening their own businesses. For these reasons, it is unlikely that much of the initial spurt of economic development will come in the form of private ownership.[6]

However, once the cycle has been put into motion, the importance and viability of private ownership increases. Many tribes have been successful with tribal enterprises. The Navajo in particular are now strenuously emphasizing the importance of private ownership and entrepreneurship.[7]

As education levels rise and the experience of the population increases, the likelihood of successful entrepreneurship increases. As individual tribal members gain expertise working in the tribal enterprises, they begin to dream of new and innovative businesses, which of course follows the development paradigm. This will lead to the growth of specialized retail services, as well as offshoots from the manufacturing enterprises.

Ronald Trosper (1992) discusses the relationship between culture and business structure. In some instances, the cultural norms may point to tribal enterprises and in other instances, sole proprietorships may be more appropriate. This is a further example of the compatibility between cultural subsystems in my social theory framework. The following two examples point toward Trosper's concept of culturally compatible enterprise.

An ongoing project of CAIED is a community development plan for a Hopi village. One of the dimensions of the overall community plan is the potential development of a cooperative buying enterprise. Many village inhabitants travel ninety miles into Flagstaff to purchase household staples and paper goods. Thus the village administration is trying to determine the viability of purchasing these goods in bulk with a cooperative enterprise.

In most other communities, the question would be simple. If the demand for products were such that an entrepreneur could earn a profit, then a business would be created. The entrepreneur would require an investment of a pickup truck and some seed funding for initial inventory. Once a track record was established, orders and even prepayments would be made. The business would flourish and grow.

But this is not a community in which such activity is likely to occur.

Following Trosper's argument, the Hopi culture does not support entrepreneurial activity. When this issue was brought up in CAIED discussions, it was quickly pointed out that any such enterprising individual would be "scorned" for trying to make money from neighbors. The intricate nature of the Hopi culture involves the complex relationships between clans and the importance of the village. As such, entrepreneurial activity, especially that aimed at "taking advantage" of neighbors, is not culturally likely.

The second example of entrepreneurial potential involves the arts and crafts market on the Navajo Reservation. For many years the arts and crafts market has been located at the Little Colorado River pull-off area on Highway 64 on the way to the Grand Canyon. This is a collection of kiosks and portable toilets. I discussed the growth of this market in an article entitled "The Issue of Compatibility between Cultural Integrity, and Economic Development among Native American Tribes" (1994b). The intersecting entrepreneurial activities that make this market workable are interesting.

The families running the individual kiosks in many instances are jewelers who make their own crafts; other individuals, however, make most of the inventory. In a sense, the family running the kiosk is the retailer. They purchase or take on consignment goods made by Navajo artisans and sell them to tourists on their way to and from the Grand Canyon.

But the market is more complex than that. The retailer also acts as wholesaler and input buyer. Traveling buyers negotiate bulk purchases from the retailer-wholesaler and simultaneously sell beads and other inputs to the kiosk retailer–wholesaler. In this sense, the kiosk retailer is the intermediate buyer and seller in both directions. My own observation is that these transactions can become quite complex, since these are essentially barter trades.

These two examples point toward Trosper's ideas of cultural compatibility and entrepreneurial activity. Stephen Cornell and Joseph Kalt (1992a) discuss a similar compatibility regarding the Oglala Sioux and the White Mountain Apache Tribes. Whereas Hopi culture does not necessarily support entrepreneurial activity, Navajo culture does support it. Navajo entrepreneurs include the kiosk retailers and the artisans and jewelers.[8]

ENTERPRISE BOARDS

For any development process to succeed, stability within the tribal government and between the tribe and outside businesses—whether they are partners, lenders, or clients—must be present. Andrew Purkey (1988) details the difficulties of tribal instability within the Crow Tribe of Montana. Joseph Kalt (1987) discusses the productivity of stable tribal governments within the White Mountain Apache and the Mescalaro Apache Tribes.

Tribal stability is vital during any planning and negotiation period. If the makeup and orientation of the tribal government change during the planning process, finalizing any project becomes difficult, and it may even be necessary to go back to the drawing board. Similarly, once negotiations have been completed and the enterprise is under way, instability within the government can lead to disturbances with the activity of the enterprise if the new government interferes with the ongoing project.

Michael Cameron (1988) emphasizes the importance of having a separation between the EDC (Economic Development Corporation) management and the political whims of government. Robert White (1990) repeatedly mentions the dual importance of a stable government and a separation between politics and day-to-day management decisions of the enterprises. Clearly, elected officials and their constituents need to be involved in long-term strategic planning, but employment and management need to be based on the productivity and profitability of the enterprise, not the political whims of the tribal council. All four reservations studied by White display a stable government.

Regardless of the forked-tongue aspect of past treaties and negotiations, tribes entering into agreements for funding, land, or supply must honor those agreements. This does not mean clauses cannot be written into contracts preventing renegotiation at some future time; rather, once a contract has been entered into, all future governments must honor that contract.

This, of course, is a partial definition of self-determination: the tribe must be accountable for its own actions. With stable government and detailed analysis, the tribe will be able to develop a detailed plan for progress. Rather than accept BIA-negotiated contracts, such as the Peabody Coal contract with the Hopi and Navajo, that subsequently lead to conflict and turmoil, the tribe itself determines its best interest and negotiates from a position of stability and knowledge. Once the negotiations are completed, it is in the best interest of the tribe that future governments honor those contracts. The success of tribal EDCs is varied. Cameron (1988) provides a detailed discussion of a prototypical EDC. The purpose of this section is to deliberate on the feasibility and practicality of an EDC on the Rosebud Sioux or similar reservation.

An EDC provides oversight of tribal enterprises. As such, it acts much like a central planning board for economic activity. Two comparisons are helpful at this point—the grandiose planning boards of the collapsed Soviet Union and the managed trade of the Japanese. Given the relatively small scale of the EDC in question, the congestion of information problems of the Soviet Union are unlikely. Instead, the developing economy of Japan in the 1950s, 1960s, and 1970s is a more relevant model of industrial policy for Native Americans today. In addition, given the use of tribal lands in activities such as hunting, fishing, and aquaculture there needs to be tribal oversight.

An EDC is most likely to be productive for a tribe beginning from the ground up. Tribes such as the Navajo, White Mountain Apache, and Mescalaro Apache have made very productive use of the EDC concept. The developing tribe should consolidate its development strategies and make formal use of an EDC, which will allow it to assimilate the necessary resource information, employment records and needs, delivery and transportation needs, and common management requirements. The EDC will also facilitate working with off-reservation businesses in the proposed joint ventures. Utilizing economies of scale, the EDC should be more productive than disparate enterprises.[9]

Caliguire and Grant (1993) discuss the importance of an enterprise board for the Hualapai Tribe. In the years following the development and implementation of the EDC, the Hualapai Tribe has utilized several of the ideas presented in this book in a variety of development projects. One of the most important aspects of the Hualapai success has been the institutional change and commitment of the tribal government.[10]

INSTITUTIONAL STRUCTURE

Cornell and Kalt have written extensively concerning the importance of institutional reform and stability in regard to the development process for Native American communities. In this section I very briefly introduce the topic.

Recent work by Rosa Gomez Dierks (1999) supports Cornell's and Kalt's viewpoints on institutional stability. Gomez Dierks, studying Latin American countries, has developed a model explaining the importance of stability and transparency in opening access to private sovereign capital markets.

Gomez Dierks extends the idea of stability by including the idea of transparency with regard to communication between governmental policy actions and private capital markets. Regardless of how stable the government is as an institutional structure, unless the government's actions are transparent to lenders, they will be unlikely to make access available. Gomez Dierks defines transparency as the willingness to make and keep commitments that private capital markets can understand and believe. For example, if the federal government is liable for absorbing the debts of state governments, then the budgeting process is not transparent when there there are institutional borders between the federal and state governments. This is similar to the importance of separating enterprises from the tribal government via an EDC, as discussed above.

Perhaps more important than simply gaining access to capital markets, Gomez Dierks's work points to the use of capital funds. Access to capital funding has a positive influence on what she calls growth-oriented expenditures on health, education, and infrastructure. She also helps confirm the conclusions in that increased exports also lead to increases in growth-oriented expenditures.

Rosa Gomez Dierks, Stephen Cornell, and Joseph Kalt are among those who argue strongly for institutional stability as a path toward economic development and self-sufficiency. Since attracting capital funding for development projects is one of the pressing issues for tribal governments, institutional stability and transparency are imperative.

CONCLUSION

This chapter has aimed at bringing together a few technical details not discussed in the previous chapters. Rather than repeat other well-written sources, I have included secondary sources in order to bring these issues to the forefront of understanding the development process. These facets need to be integrated into the development framework of the previous chapters. In the next chapter I introduce some additional aspects of community development.

NOTES

1. Timeche (1992, 1995) provides a shopping list of available resources for financial grants and loans, as well as technical assistance outlets, for Native American tribes, individuals, and Indian-owned businesses.

2. See Cecil 1988 concerning the San Carlos Apache Tribe.

3. See Kalt 1987 for a discussion of the White Mountain Apache and the Mescalaro Apache experiences with tribal enterprises. See White 1990 for the examples cited above.

4. See Cameron 1988 for a discussion of such an organization for the Crow Tribe of Montana.

5. See Brown 1990 and Cecil 1988 for discussions of this point.

6. A counterargument is appropriate at this point. Many thousands of Native Americans are entrepreneurs with their cottage industry arts and crafts and agricultural work. Although these tend to be individual or family enterprises, risk taking is inherently part of the activity. Therefore, the problems may be more correctly identified as being lack of capital funding availability and education. Joseph Anderson and I are currently working with CAIED concerning this concept.

7. Once again, this may be tribe specific. Smaller tribes may reach near full employment without developing a fully private sector. Examples of this are the White Mountain Apache and the Cochiti Pueblo.

8. This discussion does not ignore the many Hopi artisans and jewelers also involved in the arts and crafts markets.

9. See Cameron 1988 for a discussion of the vital importance of separating management of the EDC from tribal politics.

10. See Caliguire and Grant 1995 for a discussion of these changes.

12

❦

The Pernicious Triad:
Brain Drain, Dropouts,
and Joblessness

The "pernicious triad" is a well-known situation in Indian communities.[1] The economies of most communities evidence extremely high
unemployment levels, which correspond to significant shortages of
employment opportunities. The direct results of this situation form the
remaining two facets of the triad: high dropout rates and "brain drain."
Since employment opportunities are limited, many parents have only limited employment histories, and the social ills concomitant with high
unemployment rates are clearly evident to Indian youth and lead to very
substantial school dropout rates among Indian youth. Conversely, an
increasing number of Indian youth are successful in their educational
pursuits by earning various postsecondary degrees; however, since
employment possibilities in their communities are limited, a large proportion of these successful individuals are forced to find employment outside their communities. Thus the triad is formed.

The previous chapters included brief discussions of the importance of
the educational system to the overall success of development strategies.
This chapter addresses some of the problems specific to education.

THE PERNICIOUS TRIAD

Across the vastness of Canada and the United States are over five hundred Indian communities. The legal status of these communities varies
according to location, treaty status, and other issues. These communities
vary in population, land area, culture, language, resource base, proximity

to population centers (or, conversely, degree of isolation), and many other aspects. However, from as far north as Baffin Island to southern Arizona, from the eastern woods of Maine to the Pacific coastal islands of British Columbia and Alaska, these communities face similar problems. With the exception of a very few communities, primarily gaming communities, and by practically any measurement method, the economies of these communities are severely depressed. The causes and effects of poverty and other assorted ills are well documented and are probably familiar to anyone reading this book. Various measures of unemployment show rates as high as 90 percent within Indian communities.

Employment opportunities are severely limited. Those prospects that are available typically fall in two categories: government and low skill. Government employment opportunities typically involve either political appointments or a near tenure situation. Low-skill employment opportunities typically involve agriculture, resource harvesting, and construction. Limited employment opportunity is the first facet of the pernicious triad.

The limited employment situation is not a new phenomenon. (Indeed, in many communities employment options have been slowly increasing.) As a result of the past, many Indian youth come from families with little or no employment history. The consequences of continuing high unemployment rates include high rates of domestic violence, alcoholism, poverty, and the like.

Another aspect of the triad of problems involves the residential school system in both Canada and the United States. Although the conditions are improving and more local schools are being constructed, this form of education does not tend to instill a perceived benefit from education. Rarely being able to visit with family and friends, Indian youth actually see benefits from leaving school.

With few role models, little perceived benefit from education, dire social ills, and few possible or perceived employment possibilities, Indian youth have historically had very high dropout rates. In many instances, family and peer jealousies combined with adolescent preferences tend to lead students to a quick exit from school. The resulting high dropout rate is the second facet of the pernicious triad.

The above picture of Indian communities is not an attractive one; however, not all is bad. Unemployment and dropout rates have been high for many years, but recent self-determination policies in Canada and the United States have started to have the desired results: improved local economies and improved education systems. As such, more and more Indian youth are graduating from secondary school and many are earning postsecondary degrees. However, this brings the third facet of the pernicious triad into play: the issue of brain drain.

Many Indian communities are investing substantial resources in postsecondary education. Tribal colleges, scholarship programs, partnership agreements with four-year institutions, and the like result in an increased

number of Indian youth earning postsecondary degrees. However, since employment possibilities are limited within the home community, many of these highly educated individuals are forced to find employment away from their home communities. In other words, the resources devoted to education do not directly benefit the community.

This cursory description of the three facets of the pernicious triad is not meant to fully analyze the causes and effects of each problem; rather, it is meant to simply present the interactions among the facets. The next section discusses some existing and potential solutions.

POLICY REFORM

One possible policy change that would enhance the benefits of education, increasing the likelihood of students completing their education, would be to reformulate personnel policies. A council reform could make a high school diploma or equivalent a requirement for all government employment. Some Indian communities have already instituted such policies. A more specific policy would be to require a postsecondary degree for certain positions. However, one possible problem in regard to any such policy would be newly educated youth competing for jobs with individuals who may have substantial seniority in a position. This polarization could lead to fractionalization of the community.

A second partial solution would be to increase the opportunities for finishing degrees and gaining training within the communities. Workshops could be organized for specific training. Distance learning arrangements between community colleges and universities could be arranged. Interactive television broadcasting is gaining acceptance and increasing coverage. Internet-based courses are also expanding. These types of educational opportunities reduce the explicit and implicit costs of education.

The third partial solution revolves around interaction with outside corporations. Some Indian communities have the opportunity of serving as dormitory communities for proximate employment centers. For example, several pueblo communities in New Mexico are within easy commuting distance of Albuquerque. In these cases a major employment agreement can be negotiated between a corporation and an Indian community. (An example would be between the pueblo government and Intel in Albuquerque.) Other communities can negotiate agreements with, typically extractive, corporations such that a certain percentage of the local employment would necessitate hiring community members. The latter type of agreement is quite common.

However, anecdotal evidence seems to show that the agreements are weak from the Indian side of the equation or are frequently broken. Therefore, it is necessary to improve and enforce the agreements. In order to do so, it would be necessary to improve the levels of understanding between the parties and for the Indian community to negotiate from a position of increased power.

One method of increasing the level of understanding between parties would be to invite corporate participation in conferences such as the one at Colorado State. For example, a representative from the Bank of Montreal, Ron Jamieson, made a presentation concerning his company's Aboriginal Banking program. Other corporate representatives could be involved and educated concerning the issues involving Indian communities.

POSSIBLE TRIAD SOLUTIONS

The following section presents existing and possible solutions to the triad. They are presented without any implied order of importance or potential.

The National Aboriginal Apprentice Program in Canada is designed to provide internships for Indian students. This is a useful program, and similar ones exist in the United States—particularly in the national laboratories. However, the programs can be improved.

The internship programs represent the first steps toward solving the triad. Actually, they may tend to increase the brain drain aspect, since interns are often offered full-time positions at locations outside their Indian community. Countering this argument is the realization that Indian communities should not be constrained by the legal boundaries of the community. As previously discussed, if employment opportunities are available outside the legal boundary, but the individual is still able to be an active member of the community, then this should not be necessarily considered brain drain. As such, the internship programs and agreements with corporations can be improved.

One way of improving the partnerships between Indian communities and corporations would be to help in the education and acculturation of the corporate representatives. For example, corporate leaders could be invited for an extended visit to the community. Meeting with community leaders, educators, and citizens in a series of meetings and recreational events will provide corporate leaders with a realistic vantage point from which to negotiate. It is well understood among Indian leaders that non-Indians often have distorted views of Indian communities. Clearing up these misconceptions can be accomplished by inviting a small contingent of corporate leaders to actually experience, in a limited manner, the problems, issues, concerns, and lives in Indian communities.

Providing a real-life background to the conditions in and the issues of Indian communities can improve the negotiating position of the community. Once the corporate leaders are familiar with the extreme importance of a few jobs or some additional educational opportunities, they may be more willing to provide those opportunities. When the corporate leaders see and understand the importance of cultural integrity and the vibrancy of the community, they may be more willing to engage in frank and forth-right negotiations instead of taking an opportunistic stance.

In conjunction with corporate visits, Indian communities can borrow from corporate knowledge. From personnel manuals to accounting information systems to procurement procedures, corporate partners can help Indian communities develop their management systems. Again, this type of partnership can lead to a better understanding between the corporate partner and the Indian community. Although not all corporate management systems may be appropriate for a community government, some of the more technical systems can be borrowed and applied.

One method of accomplishing these combined goals would be the formation of an executive exchange partnership. An agreement could be entered that matches tribal leaders with corporate leaders. The matched pair would then spend, say, a week working together in the community atmosphere and then a week working in the corporate atmosphere. Extending this concept, lower-level community and corporate employees could work within the exchange program. Combining the exchange program with the intern program, Indian and non-Indian interns could be offered simultaneous internships that allow students to work half a semester in the corporate world and half a semester in the Indian community.

An extended exchange program could have many benefits. Corporate representatives would be able to share the knowledge and experience of the corporate world, and Indian leaders would provide insight into stewardship and resource management. The linkage between the corporate partner and the Indian community, therefore, has great potential.

The partnership between corporate and community parties can be instituted as an initial step in a joint venture. For example, an Indian community may be negotiating with a timber company concerning harvesting the forest. Working with the corporate leadership, possibly involving an exchange program, the Indian leadership can begin getting the community involved in the planning process.

It is important for the community to be kept constantly informed of the planning process. Although this may vary with the size of the population, community meetings, local newspapers or newsletters, and the like can be utilized to keep the people involved and informed. Anecdotal evidence shows that keeping the negotiations secret, either purposely or inadvertently, can lead to social unrest when the finished plan is made public. When the negotiations include an exchange program, internships, and the like, which are made public, then the community will presumably be more likely to approve the final plans.

Another facet of the negotiations involves the formulation of the joint venture. Both Canada and the United States require majority Indian ownership for various reasons. This can be problematic for many Indian communities when the joint venture is a capital-intensive operation such as forestry. The corporation will invest several tens or hundreds of thousands of dollars in equipment, but the Indian community does not have the matching capital funds available.

One creative method utilized by the Clayoquot Sound Central Region in a negotiation was to invest in "in-kind equity." During the negotiations, the community was able to account for personnel time and other activities in such a manner that they were able to make a 70 percent contribution toward their 51 percent ownership.

One of the areas of expertise in which the community can add to its in-kind equity is the use of traditional knowledge in the management of the joint venture. Traditional values, local knowledge, and traditional science can be used to adjust corporate values and procedures to improve the enterprise. For example, local knowledge of soil drainage combined with traditional science concerning forest stewardship can be used to develop more sustainable and profitable harvesting schedules. The provision of this knowledge can be "costed out" to increase the in-kind equity.

The in-kind equity approach can also be used to provide training to non-Indian corporate employees. This can be one way to avoid the humorous "Sockeye Sue" syndrome. Traditional technical and cultural knowledge can be used to avoid a situation in which the so-called expert treats each and every salmon as a sockeye. Merging mainstream and traditional science can lead to an improved enterprise.

Utilizing traditional knowledge also allows the Indian community to negotiate from a position of improved power. Apart from the ownership of the raw materials, the local knowledge adds to the mix. The threat of withholding this knowledge provides the Indian leadership with an additional negotiating point.

One last aspect of a joint enterprise with an outside corporation would involve a targeted scholarship program. It is common for corporations to target enterprise-specific scholarships involving forestry, mining, and engineering. These scholarship programs are very beneficial; however, more can be negotiated. A scholarship program could be negotiated to include the enterprise-specific scholarship and some additional community-determined scholarships. For example, the scholarship could include five scholarships for nursing and teacher education.

Apart from negotiating joint ventures, the working group also identified strategic planning as an umbrella area for focus in the war against the pernicious triad. Strategic planning within the local community can help identify and stimulate areas for development. Strategic planning can create formal and workable policies to create employment possibilities and therefore stimulate educational motivation and the desire to return to the community.

One important aspect of strategic planning is to develop policies that stimulate and afford entrepreneurial activities. Encouraging private Indian-owned business accomplishes several possibilities. These businesses could privatize some tribal government activities. One example might be trash pickup. Another possible type of business involves revitalizing or adapting traditional economic activity to modern activities. An example of this is marketing smoked salmon on a national level. A third type of entrepreneurial activity involves vertical integration. For example, a local entrepreneur could start a cabinet-making enterprise utilizing locally produced lumber.

Another aspect of the strategic planning process is to identify areas necessary for training. For example, if policies are enacted to stimulate entrepreneurial activities, it may be necessary to provide various technical assistance programs such as business plan preparation, the development of marketing plans, or the preparation of accounting statements. Another aspect of the strategic planning process is to identify consulting outlets that can provide the necessary technical assistance.[2]

An additional idea is to develop a database to act as a clearinghouse for Indian-based information. The database would include employment opportunities, training and workshop information, technical assistance outlets, and the like. The idea of the database had been discussed throughout the conference.

The award-winning Students in Free Enterprise (SIFE) organization at Northern Arizona University worked on a project with public school students on the Navajo Nation during the 1996–97 academic year. The SIFE students worked with elementary students on developing a business plan for (very) small businesses. The purpose of the project was to teach the importance of and opportunity for entrepreneurship. Indian schools can utilize the curriculum for this project.

Three steps toward accomplishing these projects and tasks are (1) reeducating and unlearning, (2) funding, and (3) educating non-Indians. Reeducation concerning potential for education and the importance of culture can attack the pernicious triad at its very heart. Unlearning the stereotypes associated with Indians is also vitally important. Reeducation regarding the possibilities for job creation and entrepreneurship can strike a devastating blow to the triad. Unlearning the supposed fact that Indians cannot be entrepreneurial because of the communal nature of Indian societies creates the potential for growth.

Funding the various projects described above is important. Whether these funds come from government sources, profits from joint ventures, or other sources is open for exploration.

Using an exchange program in conjunction with an elders program will help to educate corporate partners concerning the issues and concerns of Indian communities. Instead of viewing Indian communities as opportunities for exploitation, corporate leaders can learn the profitability potentials of partnership. This education process can be advanced by inviting corporate leaders to Indian-oriented conferences such as the one at Colorado State University.

CONCLUSION

In this chapter I do not pretend to present specific solutions to the pernicious triad of problems facing Indian communities. Rather, I have summarized a discussion that focused on these problems. The well-recognized trio of problems creates a vicious cycle, with the lack of employment opportunities driving up the dropout rates and leading to brain drain of those individuals who complete an education. The lack of a skilled workforce deters job creation and the cycle continues.

Job creation and economic development appear to be a starting place. Two avenues are open for job creation: joint ventures with outside corporations and entrepreneurial activity. In simplistic terms, improved and advanced negotiations with corporate leaders can result in more successful ventures from both sides of the negotiation. Improved understanding of the needs and knowledge of the Indian community can lead the corporate leadership into a more favorable negotiating position. Similarly, the use of traditional knowledge and culture provides an improved position for the Indian community. The net result of this improved understanding is an improved profitability and employment potential.

Providing formal and workable processes by which community members can engage in entrepreneurial activities can also lead to improved employment opportunities. Redeveloping the traditional economic activities, with adaptations incorporating modern technology, provides opportunities for income and self-sufficiency. Increased entrepreneurial opportunities will tend to bring community members back home. Individuals who have secondary diplomas and postsecondary degrees with work experience will view the new opportunities with hope. Similarly, or alternatively, the joint venture activities will also tend to bring community members back home.

The development of employment opportunities will then create a stimulus for completing the educational process. This will be particularly true when employment policies require educational achievement. More young people will see the need to finish high school. More former dropouts will see the need to complete their high school equivalencies. Interim training and technical assistance programs need to be developed to begin the entrepreneurial activities.

I recognize that eliminating the pernicious triad will involve a lengthy time period. However, the process needs to begin. The downward spiral of our Indian communities is directly linked to the pernicious triad. The processes and policies described in this chapter are initial steps in breaking those links.

NOTES

1. The material in this chapter stems from discussions held at the Math, Science, and Technology in Service of American Indian Communities Conference at Colorado State University, June 6–9, 1997. The main participants in the development of this material were Clifford Atleo Sr., Clayoquot Sound Central Region, B.C., Lillian Dyck, University of Saskatchewan, Oscar Kawagley, University of Alaska–Fairbanks, Nimke Lavelle, York University, and James Lujan, Southwest Indian Polytechnic.

2. Some examples are the National Executive Education Program for Native American Leadership, the Center for American Indian Economic Development, the Council of Energy Resource Tribes, and the National Center for American Indian Enterprise Development.

13

❧

Some Intermediate
Thoughts and Hopes

Several years have passed since that seemingly glorious day in 1992 when the agreement in principle between the Navajos and the Hopis was announced. But the dispute remains unresolved. During those years much has happened in Indian Country. Elections have been won and lost. Neither President Peterson Zah nor Chairman Vernon Masayesva holds office today. Businesses have opened, and some have closed. Plans have been made and some have been put into action. Conferences have been held. Books and articles have been published. Scholarships have been granted and students have graduated to go on to important positions in tribal governments. Children have been born. And elders have passed on.

Yet during those same years much has not happened. Although some Indian communities have had success with gaming operations and others have had success with a variety of business enterprises, the sad truth is that the Native American population as a whole is still at the bottom of the social ladder. Poverty, unemployment and underemployment, alcoholism, diabetes, spousal and child abuse, and teen suicide are still rampant problems among Native Americans.

And thus the title of this chapter. I am not proposing a panacea to all the problems facing Native Americans. Rather, I offer this chapter as an additional paddle to help the canoe fight against the strong current. In this chapter I conclude the current volume with some thoughts and hopes for the next steps.

The conferences, workshops, research, and consulting conducted by the National Executive Education Program for Native American Leadership (NEEPNAL) and the Center for American Indian Economic Development (CAIED) have helped selected tribes and businesses with their various development projects and institutional undertakings. I and many others have published interesting and useful books and articles. But much is left undone.

OLD FRIENDS AT PEACH SPRINGS

Beginning in 1989, I have had a very pleasant and productive relationship with the people of the Hualapai Nation.[1] This relationship has involved both formal and informal interaction with tribal representatives.

Upon first driving into Peach Springs, Arizona, the tribal headquarters and main community for the Hualapai Nation, in 1989, I had the impression of a dusty desert community in the process of dissolving back into the desert.

The local "restaurant" had recently closed and the non-Indian economic development planner had contacted CAIED to investigate options for reopening the enterprise. It turned out that the restaurant was located in a rather decrepit trailer with some old equipment and mismatched kitchen chairs and tables. The previous entrepreneur has simply decided one day that the business was not profitable and walked away.

The quick tour of "downtown" Peach Springs showed more aged buildings in various stages of abandonment and disrepair, a grocery store with more bare shelves than filled ones, and a gas station. After a morning of meetings and inspections, we made a roughly twelve-mile trip into Truxton for lunch.

The story goes that the day the ribbon was cut on Interstate 40 at 3:00 P.M., Peach Springs had dried up by 5:00 P.M. Long a bustling travel stop on historic Route 66, Peach Springs had flourished with several gas stations, motels, and other facilities for travelers. Bruce Babbitt (1992) says that northern Arizona is populated by towns that are mistakes: every forty miles along the Santa Fe railroad, a water stop had to be constructed and these water stops became communities. However, there really is no reason for the communities to be there at present. Peach Springs is one of those water stops. So when an alternative east-west travel route opened, the community rapidly deteriorated.

Such was the case in 1989. Few jobs, deteriorating infrastructure and buildings, non-Indian advisers, and little hope of much except reopening a failed restaurant.

In 1992, the economic development planner for the Hualapai Nation contacted CAEID again. Joe Flies-Away (1992) had recently graduated from Stanford and had returned home to Peach Springs, where he was hired as the EDA planner.

Upon driving into Peach Springs, I saw that things had changed. A sizable housing development had sprung up. More importantly, a new sense of optimism was in the air.

Following constitutional reform and new elections, attention had turned from reopening a failed business to creating a vision for a newly vitalized community and putting that vision into a development plan. The optimism was infectious, and several months later a complex community development plan was completed.[2]

In 1994, Joe Flies-Away and Waylon Honga were attending a NEEP-NAL workshop at NAU when they were called back to Peach Springs. Waylon, a recent NAU graduate, had become Joe's assistant and Joe had been elected to the tribal council. Joe and Waylon briefly explained that there was a problem with putting the development plan into action, and they left.

CAIED and NEEPNAL continued to work with the Hualapai Nation on various aspects of their development projects. Following a trip to southern Nevada, Route 66 called to me on my return to Flagstaff. Topping the hill, I noticed that the horizon was different. A new aqua-colored roof crowned the Peach Springs "skyline."

Waylon, now the enterprise director and newly elected council member (Joe had returned to law school), explained that the new motel had opened the previous month and the restaurant was scheduled to open the following month. We had lunch in the newly remodeled and now fully stocked grocery store. The tribal administration building had been remodeled and Waylon said that the Grand Canyon West[3] enterprise was flourishing.

Building the motel had required removing many of the old buildings, and the downtown area had been cleaned up. Increasing interest in the history of Route 66 had stimulated increased tourist traffic. Hualapai Riverrunners was seeing increased business for its Colorado River raft trips through the Grand Canyon. In other words, the Hualapai Nation was realizing its vision of moving toward a prosperous future.

This does not mean that all is well and done. As at Rosebud, a couple of successful small businesses are not sufficient to alleviate years of poverty and unemployment. But the momentum is moving in the right direction. Having an operational time horizon of twenty to thirty years, or, say, the seventh generation, allows for viewing these projects as the first small step.

More recently, as business is building and the community is healing, the Hualapai Nation has been able to turn its attention outward. In 1997 and again in 1998, Waylon returned to NAU to present his experiences with development and politics to a new class of Native American students. His new involvement has been working with other northern Arizona communities, Native and non-Native alike, in fighting a proposed development on the Grand Canyon.

The Hualapai Nation has seen substantial progress in the last ten years. Much remains uncompleted, but the future looks promising.

NEW FRIENDS AT MISHONGNOVI

In 1998, the village administrators of Mishongnovi Village approached CAIED for help in developing an action plan. The administrators of this Hopi village of roughly eight hundred people exude the same type of optimism Joe and Waylon had in the early years of the Hualapai development process.

Beginning in 1987, the Hopi central government began providing direct funding to individual villages. This funding became a formal part of the budgeting process a year later. Mishongnovi Village has used these funds for a variety of community projects over the last decade. These have included infrastructure expansion and repair, community cleanup, house painting, and the establishment of a youth program.

In 1996 a visioning process was undertaken to formulate goals for the village. As with the Hualapai experience, this document is now being implemented to initiate various community development projects.

However, the starting point of this development process is somewhat disheartening. Unlike Peach Springs, the Hopi villages are several centuries old. Whereas Peach Springs had some semblance of economic activity in recent decades, the isolation of the Hopi villages has brought little in the form of interaction with the mainstream economy until very recently.

For example, the upper village, on top of the mesa, has no water or sewer and was only partially wired for electricity in 1990. The traditional sources of water for agriculture are diminishing. And the centuries-old buildings in the upper village are in serious disrepair.

One of the new CAIED consultants was dismayed at the conditions. This was his first visit to a reservation community and he could only compare the conditions to villages he had visited in North Africa.

At this writing, the Mishongnovi project is still in the elementary stages of raw data collection. Hopefully, these first small steps will lead the residents of Mishongnovi on a path toward a successful future.

LITTLE FIRST STEPS LEAD TOWARD LARGER ONES

The comparative situations of Peach Springs and Mishongnovi illustrate the challenges still to be tackled in Indian Country. Peach Springs desired the reopening of one of three local businesses and Mishongnovi desires various facilities. These are not problems faced by the vast majority of the population in the United States.

Nor do most communities face unemployment rates in excess of 50 percent and all the concomitant social strife. However, Native American communities face these challenges every day. Tribal leaders yearn for solutions and struggle with day-to-day problems. Yet the optimism of these leaders—elected and otherwise—holds hope for the future.

Native American societies have survived centuries of external interference, disruption, conquest, and misunderstanding. Yet survive they do. In order to move from the sometimes depressing status quo to a future of prosperity and self-sufficiency, substantial changes must take place.

Understanding social and economic processes within the context of community development provides the background for those first small steps. The strategies and the examples described in earlier chapters can be used by tribal leaders to formulate their visions of the future and move toward implementation of those visions.

The end result of the strategic planning process is therefore only the initial step on the path toward self-sufficiency and self-determination, but it is a vital step. In order to take this step, the tribal community must be looking forward and must be ready to take the risks necessary to reach into the future. Creating the vision of what that future may hold is more important, perhaps, than detailing the specific activities to undertake. The economic, community, cultural, and other endeavors within the body of the plan are simply the means to the end of reaching the vision of the people.

NOTES

1. Much of this work has been proprietary in nature. As such this section only discusses publicly available information.

2. This project was the first effort at developing a plan, as discussed in chapter 8.

3. Grand Canyon West is located on the rim of the Grand Canyon. Tourists arrive, primarily from Las Vegas, by plane and bus.

References

Anderson, Joseph, and Dean Howard Smith. 1999. "Managing Tribal Assets: Developing Long-Term Strategic Plans." *American Indian Culture and Research Journal* 22, no. 2.

Anderson, Kat, and Gary Paul Nabhan. 1991. "Gardeners in Eden." *Wilderness*, Fall 1991, pp. 27–30.

Andreas, Mary Ann. 1997. Comments made at the Indian Gaming: Who Wins conference, UCLA, April 4. Andreas was tribal chairperson of the Morongo Band of Mission Indians.

Archambault, Donovan. 1992. "Drug and Alcohol Treatment." Mimeograph proposal advanced by Senator Conrad Burns (Montana). A copy is available in the appendices in Smith and Ozmun 1994.

Arizona Department of Commerce. 1990. *Arizona Community Profiles*. Phoenix: Arizona Department of Commerce.

Aveni, Anthony F. 1997. *Stairways to the Stars: Skywatching in Three Great Ancient Cultures*. New York: Wiley.

Babbitt, Bruce. 1992. Comments made at the Colorado Plateau Community Initiatives symposium, Coping with Change: Economy and Environment Conference, Cedar City, Utah.

Bailey, Ronald. 1993. *ECOSCAM: The False Prophets of Ecological Apocalypse*. New York: St. Martin's.

Bakeless, John. 1950. *The Eyes of Discovery*. New York: Lippincott.

Barkley, David L., ed. 1993. *Economic Adaptation: Alternatives for Nonmetropolitan Areas*. Boulder: Westview.

Baumol, William J., and Wallace E. Oates. 1988. *The Theory of Environmental Policy*. 2d ed. New York: Cambridge University Press.

Becker, Gary. 1971. *Economic Theory*. New York: Knopf.

Benedek, Emily. 1992. *The Wind Won't Know Me: A History of the Navaho-Hopi Land Dispute*. New York: Knopf.

Bieder, Robert E. 1986. *Science Encounters the Indians, 1820–1880: The Early Years of American Ethnology*. Norman: University of Oklahoma Press.

151

Bishop, Charles A. 1981. "Northeastern Indian Concepts of Conservation and the Fur Trade: A Critique of Calvin Martin's Thesis." In *Indians, Animals, and the Fur Trade: A Critique of Keepers of the Game*. Edited by Shepard Krech III. Athens: University of Georgia Press.

———. 1984. "The First Century: Adaptive Changes among the Western James Bay Cree between the Early Seventeenth and Early Eighteenth Centuries." In *The Subarctic Fur Trade: Native Social and Economic Adaptations*. Edited by Shepard Krech III. Vancouver: University of British Columbia Press.

Boulding, Kenneth E. 1966. "The Economics of the Coming Spaceship Earth." In *Environmental Quality in a Growing Economy*. Edited by Henry Jarrett. Baltimore: Johns Hopkins Press.

Bowannie, John. 1992. Interview by author, September. Bowannie was president of Cochiti Community Development.

Brown, Dee. 1970. *Bury My Heart at Wounded Knee: An Indian History of the American West*. New York: Holt.

Brown, John R. 1990. "Entrepreneurship Development: Thinking *Economically* Is Not Enough." Mimeograph. Navajo Nation Division of Economic Development.

Caliguire, Daria, and Kenneth Grant. 1993. *A Foundation for Economic Development for the Hualapai Nation: Building an Enterprise Board*. Cambridge: The Harvard Project on American Indian Economic Development, John F. Kennedy School of Government, April.

Cameron, Michael W. 1988. *A Prototypical Development Corporation for American Indian Tribes: A Report to the Crow Tribe of Montana*. Cambridge: The Harvard Project on American Indian Economic Development, John F. Kennedy School of Government, May.

———. 1990. *A Prototypical Economic Development Corporation for Native American Tribes*. Cambridge: The Harvard Project on American Indian Economic Development, John F. Kennedy School of Government, April.

Cecil, Kelly L. 1988. *Encouraging Entrepreneurship on the San Carlos Apache Reservation*. Cambridge: The Harvard Project on American Indian Economic Development, John F. Kennedy School of Government, May.

Chekki, Dan A. 1989. *Dimensions of Communities: A Research Handbook*. New York: Garland.

Churchill, Ward. 1997. *A Little Matter of Genocide: Holocaust and Denial in the Americas, 1492 to the Present*. San Francisco: City Lights.

Coase, Ronald H. 1988. *The Firm, the Market, and the Law*. Chicago: University of Chicago Press.

Conover, Jerry. 1988. "Indian Art and Craft Sales in the Phoenix Area: A Market Analysis." Mimeograph, Northern Arizona University, Flagstaff, Ariz.

Cornell, Stephen, and Joseph P. Kalt. 1990. "Pathways from Poverty: Economic Development and Institution-Building on American Indian Reservations." *American Indian Culture and Research Journal* 14, no. 3: 89–125.

———. 1991. *Where's the Glue? Institutional Bases of American Indian Economic Development*. Cambridge: The Harvard Project on American Indian Economic Development, John F. Kennedy School of Government, February.

———. 1992a. *Reloading the Dice: Improving the Chances for Economic Development on American Indian Reservations*. Cambridge: The Harvard Project on American Indian Economic Development, John F. Kennedy School of Government, March.

Cornell, Stephen, and Joseph Kalt, eds. 1992b. *What Can Tribes Do?* Los Angeles: University of Los Angeles Press.

Corrigan, Philip, and Derek Sayer. 1985. *The Great Arch: English State Formation as Cultural Revolution*. New York: Basil Blackwell.

Cropper, Maureen L., and Wallace E. Oates. 1992. "Environmental Economics: A Survey." *Journal of Economic Literature*, June, pp. 675–740.

Daly, Herman E. 1977. "The Steady-State Economy: What, Why, and How." In *The Sustainable Society: Implications for Limited Growth*. Edited by Dennis Clark Pirages. New York: Praeger.

Daniel, Joseph E., ed. 1993. *Ecotravel*. Boulder: Buzzworm.

Davis, H. Craig. 1990. *Regional Economic Impact Analysis and Project Evaluation*. Vancouver: University of British Columbia Press.

Davison, Don. 1992. *Southwest Sage*, December 30, p. 5.

Deloria, Vine, Jr. 1970. *We Talk, You Listen: New Tribes, New Turf*. New York: Macmillan.

———. 1995. *Red Earth, White Lies: Native Americans and the Myth of Scientific Fact*. New York: Scribner's.

Deloria, Vine, Jr., and Clifford Lytle. 1984. *The Nations Within: The Past and Future of American Indian Sovereignty*. New York: Pantheon.

De Mente, Boye. 1988. *Visitor's Guide to Arizona's Indian Reservations*. Phoenix: Phoenix Books.

DeMott, John S. 1993. "Recasting Enterprise Zones." *Nation's Business*, February, pp. 16–21.

Deresky, Helen. 1997. *International Management: Managing across Borders and Cultures*. Reading, Mass.: Addison–Wesley.

Devereux, Edward C. 1961. "Parsons' Sociological Theory." In *The Social Theories of Talcott Parsons*. Edited by Max Black. Englewood Cliffs, N J : Prentice-Hall.

Diamant, Adam. 1988. *Economic Development: The Rosebud Sioux Indian Tribe: A Report to the Rosebud Sioux Tribe*. Project Report Series 88–89. Cambridge: The Harvard Project on American Indian Economic Development, John F. Kennedy School of Government, May.

Dietz, Frank J., and Jan van der Straaten. 1992. "Rethinking Environmental Economics: Missing Links between Economic Theory and Environmental Policy." *Journal of Economic Issues*, March, pp. 27–51.

Echohawk, Larry. 1992. Speech made to the National Democratic Convention, July 16. At the time Echohawk was attorney general of Idaho.

Edgell, David L., Sr. 1992. "A Small Community Adopts Tourism as a Development Tool." *Business America*, April 20, pp. 16–20.

Edwards, David A. 1983. "The Unified Regional Approach to Community Economic Development in Today's Economy." *Governmental Finance*, December, pp. 7–12.

Ehrlich, Paul R. 1989. "Will Economists Learn to Respect Mother Nature?" *Business and Society Review*, Fall, pp. 60–63.

Enfield, Marilyn. 1992. Interview by author, April-May. Enfield was the general manager of Apache Aerospace.

Festa, David H., and James St. George. 1988. *Evaluation of Reservation–Based Loan Programs*. Cambridge: The Harvard Project on American Indian Economic Development, John F. Kennedy School of Government, May.

First Nations Financial Project. 1991. *First Nations Development Institute: Ten Year Report*. Falmouth, Va.

Flies-Away, Joseph. 1992. Interview by author, August. Flies-Away was tribal planner for the Hualapai Nation.

Garcia, Nora. 1992. Interview by author, June. Garcia was chairwoman of the Fort Mohave Tribe.

Glover, Glenda, and J. Paul Brownridge. 1993. "Enterprise Zones as an Investment of Urban Policy: A Review of the Zones in South Central Los Angeles." *Government Finance Review*, June, pp. 15–17.

Goforth, Gary. 1992. Interview by author, August. Goforth was tribal planner for the Fort Mohave Tribe.

Goldemberg, José, and Hal Harvey. 1997. "Next Stop: The Electric Bus." *Technology Review*, May-June, p. 67.

Gomez Dierks, Rosa. 1999. "The Political Economy of Institutional Choice: Policy Commitments and Global Finance." Ph.D. diss., Northern Arizona University.

Gore, Al. 1992. "The Unsheltering Sky." *National Parks*, July-August, pp. 26–27.

Grand Canyon Trust. 1992. *Proceedings of the Colorado Plateau Community Initiatives Symposium Coping with Change: Economy and Environment.* Flagstaff, Ariz.: Grand Canyon Trust.

Grant, Linda. 1995. "Shutting Down the Regulatory Machine." *U.S. News and World Report*, February 13, pp. 70–72.

Harris, Philip, and Robert Moran. 1991. *Managing Cultural Differences.* Houston: Gulf.

Hayden, F. Gregory. 1993. "Ecosystem Valuation: Combining Economics, Philosophy, and Ecology." *Journal of Economic Issues*, June, pp. 409–20.

Her Many Horses, Mike. 1992. Interview by author, August. Her Many Horses was executive director of the Oglala Sioux Tribe (Pine Ridge Reservation).

Hofstede, Geert. 1992. "Comparative Management in Five Cultures." Address to the national conference of the Academy of Management, Las Vegas, Nev.

Holbrook, Stewart H. 1943. *Burning an Empire: The Story of American Forest Fires.* New York: Macmillan.

Horn, Miriam, and Dana Hawkins. 1991. "America before Columbus." *U.S. News and World Report*, July 8, pp. 22–37.

Iverson, Peter. 1992. "Taking Care of the Earth and Sky." In *America in 1492: The World of the Indian Peoples before the Arrival of Columbus.* Edited by Alvin M. Josephy Jr. New York: Knopf.

Jacobs, Jane. 1984. *Cities and the Wealth of Nations.* New York: Random House.

Jeffers, Susan. 1991. *Brother Sky, Sister Eagle: A Message from Chief Seattle.* New York: Dial Books.

Jennings, Francis. 1992. "American Frontiers." In *America in 1492: The World of the Indian Peoples before the Arrival of Columbus.* Edited by Alvin M. Josephy Jr. New York: Knopf.

Jones, Lisa. 1993. "Ecotourism: Closing the Gap between Intent and Action." In *Ecotravel.* Edited by Joseph E. Daniel. Boulder: Buzzworm.

Jorgensen, Miriam. 1990a. *Nebraska Sioux Lean Beef, Part A: A Teaching Case Study in Tribal Management of Oglala Lakota College.* Teaching Case C-2. Cambridge: The Harvard Project on American Indian Economic Development, John F. Kennedy School of Government, August.

———. 1990b. *Nebraska Sioux Lean Beef, Part B: A Teaching Case Study in Tribal Management of Oglala Lakota College.* Teaching Case C-3. Cambridge: The Harvard Project on American Indian Economic Development, John F. Kennedy School of Government, August.

Josephy, Alvin M., Jr., ed. 1992. *America in 1492: The World of the Indian Peoples before the Arrival of Columbus.* New York: Knopf.

Kalt, Joseph. 1987. *The Redefinition of Property Rights in American Indian Reservations: A Comparative Analysis of Native American Economic Development.* Cambridge: The Harvard Project on American Indian Economic Development, John F. Kennedy School of Government, May.

Krech, Shepard, III, ed. 1981. *Indians, Animals, and the Fur Trade: A Critique of Keepers of the Game.* Athens: University of Georgia Press.

———. 1984. *The Subarctic Fur Trade: Native Social and Economic Adaptations.* Vancouver: University of British Columbia Press.

Krepps, Matthew B. 1991. *Can Tribes Manage Their Own Resources? A Study of American Indian Forestry and the 638 Program.* Cambridge: The Harvard Project on American Indian Economic Development, John F. Kennedy School of Government, November.

Lopach, James J., Margery Hunter Brown, and Richmond L. Crow. 1990. *Tribal Government Today: Politics on Montana Indian Reservations.* Boulder: Westview.

Ludwig, Ann, and Jim Schowalter. 1988. *Financing American Indian Economic Development: An Analysis and Organizational Structure for S. 271: The Indian Development Finance Corporation Act.* Cambridge: The Harvard Project on American Indian Economic Development, John F. Kennedy School of Government, April.

MacLiesh, William H. 1991. "From Sea to Shining Sea: 1492." *Smithsonian*, November, pp. 34–49.

Martin, Calvin. 1978. *Keepers of the Game: Indian–Animal Relationships and the Fur Trade.* Berkeley: University of California Press.

———. 1981. "The War between Indians and Animals." In *Indians, Animals, and the Fur Trade: A Critique of Keepers of the Game.* Edited by Shepard Krech III. Athens: University of Georgia Press.

Masayesva, Vernon. 1991. Comments made at the National Native American Business Organization conference, Flagstaff, Ariz., November 8. Masayesva was chairman of the Hopi Tribe.

Matthiessen, Peter. 1991. *In the Spirit of Crazy Horse.* New York: Viking.

Medicine Crow, Joseph. 1992. *From the Heart of the Crow Country: The Crow Indians' Own Stories.* New York: Orion.

Mike, Richard. 1992. Comments made at the American Indian Opportunity Day, sponsored by the National Center for American Indian Enterprise and Development, Phoenix, January.

Momaday, N. Scott. 1970. "An American Land Ethic." In *Ecotactics: The Sierra Club Handbook for Environmental Activists.* Edited by John G. Mitchell. New York: Simon & Schuster.

———. 1991. "Confronting Columbus Again." In *Native American Testimony.* Edited by Peter Nabokov. New York: Viking Penguin. Originally published as "Viewing the Shore: American Indian Perspectives on the Quintcentenary." *Northeast Indian Quarterly*, Fall 1990.

Monrad, Marie. 1988. *Native American Tribal Trust Funds: Expanding Options for Tribal Control.* Cambridge: The Harvard Project on American Indian Economic Development, John F. Kennedy School of Government, April.

Morse, Chandler. 1961. "The Functional Imperatives." In *The Social Theories of Talcott Parsons.* Edited by Max Black. Englewood Cliffs, N.J.: Prentice-Hall.

Mowat, Farley. [1973] 1989. *Ordeal by Ice.* Toronto: McClelland & Stewart.

Mt. Pleasant, Jane. 1997. Comments made to the Math, Science, and Technology Education in Service of Indian Communities conference at Colorado State University, June 6.

Murray, Charles. 1984. *Losing Ground: American Social Policy, 1950–1980*. New York: Basic.

Nabokov, Peter, ed. 1991. *Native American Testimony*. New York: Viking Penguin.

Nissenbaum, Paul, and Paul Shadle. 1992. "Building a System for Land Use Planning: A Case Study for the Puyallup Tribe." In *What Can Tribes Do?* Edited by Stephen Cornell and Joseph Kalt. Los Angeles: University of Los Angeles Press.

Norgaard, Richard B. 1988. "The Rise of the Global Exchange Economy and the Loss of Biological Diversity." In *Biodiversity*. Edited by E. O. Wilson. Washington, D.C.: National Academy Press.

———. 1994. *Development Betrayed: The End of Progress and a Coevolutionary Revisioning of the Future*. New York: Routledge.

North, Douglass C. 1988. "Institutions, Transaction Costs, and Economic Growth." *Economic Inquiry*, July, pp. 419–28.

OECD "Economics and the Environment: Not Conflict but Symbiosis." 1984. *Observer*, September, pp. 30–34.

Parsons, Talcott. 1957. *Economy and Society*. Glencoe, Ill.: Free Press.

Perry, James A., and Robert K. Dixon. 1986. "An Interdisciplinary Approach to Community Resource Management: Preliminary Field Test in Thailand." *Journal of Developing Ideas*, October, pp. 31–47.

Pirages, Dennis Clark. 1977a. "Introduction: A Social Design for Sustainable Growth." In *The Sustainable Society: Implications for Limited Growth*. New York: Praeger.

Pirages, Dennis Clark, ed. 1977b. *The Sustainable Society: Implications for Limited Growth*. New York: Praeger.

Plotkin, Mark J. 1993. *Tales of a Shaman's Apprentice: An Ethnobotanist Searches for New Medicines in the Amazon Rain Forest*. New York: Viking.

Pomice, Eva, and Dana Hawkins. 1992. "Delivering the Goods." *U.S. News and World Report*, July 13, pp. 51–52.

Presidential Commission on Indian Reservation Economics. 1984. *Report and Recommendations to the President of the United States*. November. 851-J-3. Washington, D.C.: GPO.

Purkey, Andrew. 1988. *The Crow Tribal Government and Economic Development*. Cambridge: The Harvard Project on American Indian Economic Development, John F. Kennedy School of Government, May.

Ramirez, Heriberto. 1992. Comments made at the American Indian Opportunity Day, sponsored by the National Center for American Indian Enterprise and Development, Phoenix, January.

Ray, Arthur J. 1984. "Periodic Shortages, Native Welfare, and the Hudson's Bay Company, 1670–1930." In *The Subarctic Fur Trade: Native Social and Economic Adaptations*. Edited by Shepard Krech III. Vancouver: University of British Columbia Press.

Reed, Smith, Shaw, and McClay 1991. "Pilot Mentor–Protégé Program." Mimeograph, McClean, Va. Contact the authors at 703–556–8440.

Richardson, Boyce. 1993. *People of Terra Nullius: Betrayal and Rebirth in Aboriginal Canada*. Vancouver: Douglas & McIntyre.

Ridington, Robin. 1992. "Northern Hunters." In *America in 1492*. Edited by Alvin M. Josephy Jr. New York: Knopf.

Schelling, Thomas C. 1992. "Some Economics of Global Warming." *American Economic Review*, March pp. 1–14.

Smith, Adam. [1776] 1987. *The Wealth of Nations*. London: Penguin.

Smith, Dean Howard. 1994a. "Native American Economic Development: A Modern Approach." *Review of Regional Studies* 24, no. 1: 87–102.

———. 1994b. "The Issue of Compatibility between Cultural Integrity, and Economic Development among Native American Tribes." *American Indian Culture and Research Journal*, Fall, pp. 177–206.

———. 1994c. "An Integrated Approach to Community Development: The Case of the Fort Belknap Indian Community." Mimeograph. Available from the author.

———. 1994d. Review of Plotkin's *Tales of a Shaman's Apprentice. American Indian Culture and Research Journal* 18, no. 2: 212–15.

Smith, Dean Howard, and Jon Ozmun. 1994. *Fort Belknap's Community Development Plan: A Teaching Case Study in Tribal Management*. Teaching Case C–5. Cambridge: The Harvard Project on American Indian Economic Development, John F. Kennedy School of Government, May.

Smith, Michael E. 1997. "Life in the Provinces of the Aztec Empire." *Scientific American*, September, pp. 76–83.

Steele, John Yellow Bird. 1992. Interview by author, August. Steele was president of the Oglala Sioux Tribe (Pine Ridge Reservation).

Stigler, George J. 1966. *The Theory of Price*. 3d ed. New York: Macmillan.

Taylor, Colin F, and William C. Sturtevant. 1991. *The Native Americans: The Indigenous People of North America*. New York: Smithmark.

Taylor, Don, and Carlton Owen. 1991. "Balancing Economics and the Environment." *Journal of Forestry*, November, pp. 13–16.

Thistle, Paul C. 1986. *Indian–European Trade Relations in the Lower Saskatchewan River Region to 1840*. Winnipeg: University of Manitoba Press.

Thomas, David Hurst. 1994. *Exploring Ancient Native America: An Archaeological Guide*. New York: Macmillan.

Tiebout, Charles. 1962. *The Community Economic Base Study*. New York: Committee for Economic Development.

Timeche, Joan. 1992, 1995. *Resources for American Indian Economic Development Projects and Businesses*. Flagstaff: Northern Arizona University Press.

Tocqueville, Alexis de. [1835] 1966. *Democracy in America*. Edited by J. P. Mayer and Max Lerner. Translated by George Lawrence. New York: Harper & Row.

Trosper, Ronald L. 1992. "Mind Sets and Economic Development on Indian Reservations." In *What Can Tribes Do?* Edited by Stephen Cornell and Joseph Kalt. Los Angeles: University of Los Angeles Press.

U.S. Congress. Senate. Select Committee on Indian Affairs. 1989. *Final Report and Legislative Recommendations*. November.

U.S. Department of the Interior. 1986. *Report of the Task Force on Indian Economic Development*. July.

Vizenor, Erma J. 1997. Comments made at the Indian Gaming: Who Wins conference at UCLA, April 4. Vizenor is a tribal councilperson on the White Earth Reservation.

Ward, Barbara. 1962. *The Rich Nations and the Poor Nations*. New York: Norton.

Warden, Howard T., II, 1966. *Native Inheritance*. New York: Harper & Row.

Washburn, Wilcomb E. 1973. *The American Indian and the United States: A Documentary History*. Vols. 1–4. Westport, Conn.: Greenwood.

Weatherford, Jack. 1991. *Native Roots: How the Indians Enriched America*. New York: Fawcett.

White, Robert H. 1990. *Tribal Assets: The Rebirth of Native America*. New York: Holt.

Wilson, E. O. 1988. *Biodiversity*. Washington, D.C.: National Academy Press.

Wright, Ronald. 1992. *Stolen Continents: The Americas through Indian Eyes since 1492*. New York: Houghton Mifflin.

Yazzie, R. 1989. "Convenience Stores: The Third Wave of Navajo Retail Outlets." *Navajo Nation Economic Development Forum*, November-December.

Zah, Peterson. 1993. Comments made at the Reservation Economic Summit '93, Phoenix, June. At the time Zah was president of the Navajo Nation.

Subject Index

40–41; historical, 3, 7; intentions of, 35; land allotments, 36; and resource acquisition, 39; right of conquest, 34; and sovereignty, 36, 39–40; treaties in, 34. *See also* assimilation; Bureau of Indian Affairs

financial subsystems, role in development plan, 98–99

fires, controlled, 28

First Nations Financial Project, 73, 126

fisheries, salmon, 15, 79, 88

Flies-Away, Joseph, 147

forest management: in Amazon Rain forest, 88; pre-contact, 28, 78

Forest Products Enterprise, 107

Fort Belknap Agency, 114

Fort Belknap Indian Community, 97; alcoholism at, 114–15; community action plan, 117–19; economic subsystem, changes in, 116–17; import earning activities, 115–16; main industry, 114; overview of, 114–15; present enterprises at, 114; proposed alcohol treatment centers, 118–21; thinning/reforestation programs at, 115, 118; unemployment at, 114, 115

Fort McDowell Yavapai Indian Community, 127

Fort Mojave Reservation, 53

Franklin, Benjamin, 41, 61

funding opportunities, capital: bonds, 125; business site leases, 63, 124–25; loans, 124–25; partnerships with outside firms, 73, 124; trusts, 73; venture capital, 125

fur trade, 80–81

Gallatin, Albert, 30–31

Garcia, Nora, 64

General Allotment Act (1887), 35, 40

genocide. *See* extermination

global economy, influence of Native principles in, 79–80

Grand Traverse Band, 18

Grant administration, 35, 40

Gros Ventre Tribe, 114

Hantavirus, 87

Harmony, Navajo concept of, 82

Harvard Project on American Indian Economic Development, xii, 4

Havasupai Tribe, 13–14, 67, 79

Henry Hudson, 26–27

Homestead Act, 82

Honga, Waylon, 147

Hopewell culture: decline of, 24, 26; trade networks, precontact, 23–24, 29

Hopi, 38; development at Mishongnovi Village, 148; and Navajo-Hopi land dispute, 1–2; rejection of mainstream economic development, 13–14, 67; traditional government, 41–42. *See also* Peabody Coal

Hopi Technologies, 128

House Concurrent Resolution, 36, 40

H.R. 1022, 86, 88

Hualapai: enterprise board, 132; government employment of, 53; potential for economic development of, 73; recent economic enterprise at, 146–48; rejection of mainstream economic development, 13–14, 67

Hudson, Henry, 26–27

IBM, 128

import replacement: multiplier effect in, 49–50; role in sustained development, 47–48; stage in economic growth, 46

Indian, federal qualification, 6

Indian Civil Rights Act, 36–37, 39

Indian Claims Commission, 36, 39

Indian Education Act, 37, 39

Indian gaming, 38, 46, 51

Indian Removal Act (1830), 34, 40

Indian Reorganization Act (IRA), 36, 75, 96

Indian Self-Determination and Education Assistance Act, 37, 39

Indian Wars, 40

individuality, 63

internship programs, 138, 139

Author Index

Author Index

About the Author

Dean Howard Smith is associate professor of applied indigenous studies and economics. He is Mohawk. His family comes from the Grand River Reserve of the Six Nations in Ontario. He received his Ph.D. from Texas A&M University. He works with the Center for American Indian Economic Development and is on the teaching faculty of the National Executive Education Program for Native American Leadership. He is the faculty adviser for the Native American Business Organization. His publications mostly focus on economic development on Indian reservations. He has also published papers on pricing strategies and environmental issues.